Lecture Notes in Artificial Intelligence 11377

Subseries of Lecture Notes in Computer Science

Series Editors

Randy Goebel
  University of Alberta, Edmonton, Canada
Yuzuru Tanaka
  Hokkaido University, Sapporo, Japan
Wolfgang Wahlster
  DFKI and Saarland University, Saarbrücken, Germany

Founding Editor

Jörg Siekmann
  DFKI and Saarland University, Saarbrücken, Germany

More information about this series at http://www.springer.com/series/1244

Friedhelm Schwenker · Stefan Scherer (Eds.)

Multimodal Pattern Recognition of Social Signals in Human-Computer-Interaction

5th IAPR TC 9 Workshop, MPRSS 2018
Beijing, China, August 20, 2018
Revised Selected Papers

Springer

Editors
Friedhelm Schwenker
Ulm University
Ulm, Germany

Stefan Scherer
University of Southern California
Playa Vista, CA, USA

ISSN 0302-9743   ISSN 1611-3349   (electronic)
Lecture Notes in Artificial Intelligence
ISBN 978-3-030-20983-4   ISBN 978-3-030-20984-1   (eBook)
https://doi.org/10.1007/978-3-030-20984-1

LNCS Sublibrary: SL7 – Artificial Intelligence

This Springer imprint is published by the registered company Springer Nature Switzerland AG
The registered company address is: Gewerbestrasse 11, 6330 Cham, Switzerland

Preface

This book presents the proceedings of the 5th IAPR TC 9 Workshop on Pattern Recognition of Social Signals in Human–Computer Interaction (MPRSS 2018). This workshop endeavored to bring together recent research in pattern recognition and human–computer interaction, and succeeded to install a forum for ongoing discussions. In recent years, research in the field of intelligent human–computer interaction has made considerable progress in methodology and application. However, building intelligent artificial companions capable of interacting with humans, in the same way humans interact with each other, remains a major challenge in this field. Pattern recognition and machine learning methodology play a major role in this pioneering research. MPRSS 2018 mainly focused on pattern recognition, machine learning, and information fusion methods with applications in social signal processing, including multimodal emotion recognition and pain intensity estimation; especially the question of how to distinguish between human emotions from pain or stress induced by pain was discussed. For the MPRSS 2018 workshop nine out of 12 papers were selected for inclusion in this volume. MPRSS 2018 was held as a satellite workshop of the International Conference on Pattern Recognition (ICPR 2018) in Bejing, China, on August 20, 2018.

This workshop would not have been possible without the help of many people and organizations. First of all, we are grateful to all the authors who submitted their contributions to the workshop. We thank the members of the Program Committee for performing the difficult task of selecting the best papers for this book, and we hope that readers of this volume will enjoy this selection of excellent papers and be inspired from its contributions. MPRSS 2018 was supported by the University of Ulm (Germany), the University of Southern California (USA), the International Association for Pattern Recognition (IAPR), and the new IAPR Technical Committee on Pattern Recognition in Human–Computer Interaction (TC 9). Finally, we wish to express our gratitude to Springer for their patience and for publishing our workshop proceedings in their LNCS/LNAI series.

March 2019

Friedhelm Schwenker
Stefan Scherer

Organization

Organizing Committee

Friedhelm Schwenker   Ulm University, Germany
Stefan Scherer   University of Southern California, USA

Program Committee

Hazem M. Abbas   Ain Shams University Cairo, Egypt
Shigeo Abe   Kobe University, Japan
Amir Atiya   Cairo University, Egypt
Nadia Mana   Fondazione Bruno Kessler, Italy
Mariofanna Milanova   University of Arkansas at Little Rock, USA
Günther Palm   Ulm University, Germany
Stefan Scherer   University of Southern California, USA
Friedhelm Schwenker   Ulm University, Germany
Eugene Semenkin   Siberian State Aerospace University, Russia

Sponsoring Institutions

International Association for Pattern Recognition (IAPR)
IAPR TC 9 on *Pattern Recognition in Human–Computer Interaction*
Ulm University, Germany
University of Southern California, USA

Contents

Multi-focus Image Fusion with PCA Filters of PCANet

Xu Song and Xiao-Jun Wu$^{(\boxtimes)}$

Jiangsu Provincial Engineering Laborator of Pattern Recognition and Computational Intelligence, Jiangnan University, Wuxi 214122, China
xiaojun_wu_jnu@163.com

Abstract. As is well known to all, the training of deep learning model is time consuming and complex. Therefore, in this paper, a very simple deep learning model called PCANet is used to extract image features from multi-focus images. First, we train the two-stage PCANet using ImageNet to get PCA filters which will be used to extract image features. Using the feature maps of the first stage of PCANet, we generate activity level maps of source images by using nuclear norm. Then, the decision map is obtained through a series of post-processing operations on the activity level maps. Finally, the fused image is achieved by utilizing a weighted fusion rule. The experimental results demonstrate that the proposed method can achieve state-of-the-art fusion performance in terms of both objective assessment and visual quality.

Keywords: Multi-focus image fusion · PCA filters · Nuclear norm

1 Introduction

Image fusion is an information fusion of images. It combines different images obtained by different sensors for the same target or scene, or different images obtained with the same sensor in different imaging modes or at different imaging times. The multi-focus image fusion is a branch of image fusion. The fused image can reflect the information of multiple original images to achieve a comprehensive description of the target and the scene, making it more suitable for visual perception or computer processing. Multi-focus image fusion has become a representative topic since many algorithms have been developed in many fields, such as remote sensing applications, medical imaging applications and surveillance applications [14]. Conventionally, the multi-focus image fusion algorithms can be divided into transform domain algorithms and spatial domain algorithms [15]. Since there are many new algorithms that have been proposed recently, we would like to divide the existing fusion algorithms into three categories: multi-scale transform methods, sparse representation (SR) and low-rank representation based fusion methods, and deep learning based fusion methods.

The multi-scale transform (MST) methods are the most commonly used methods, such as discrete wavelet transform (DWT) [9], contourlet transform

F. Schwenker and S. Scherer (Eds.): MPRSS 2018, LNAI 11377, pp. 1–17, 2019.
https://doi.org/10.1007/978-3-030-20984-1_1

(CT) [25], shift-invariant shearlet transform [24] and curvelet transform (CVT) [5] etc. The basic idea is to perform image transformation on the source images to get the coefficient representation. Then fuse the coefficients according to a certain fusion rule to obtain fused coefficients, and finally obtain the fused image through inverse transformation. All these methods share a "decomposition-fusion-reconstruction" framework. These methods are good representation of their structural information, but can only extract limited direction information and cannot accurately extract the complete contours [26].

In recent years, methods based on sparse representation and low rank representation also have significant performance in image fusion. Yin et al. [27] proposed a novel multi-focus image fusion approach. The key point of this approach is that a maximum weighted multi-norm fusion rule is used to reconstruct fused image from sparse coefficients and the joint dictionary. And the method based on saliency detection in sparse domain [16] also has a remarkable result. Yang el al. [26] combined robust sparse representation with adaptive PCNN is also an effective method. Liu et al. [20] combined multi-scale transform with sparse representation for image fusion which overcomes the inherent defects of both the MST- and SR-based fusion methods. Besides the above methods, Li et al. [10] proposed a novel multi-focus image fusion method based on dictionary learning and low-rank representation which gets a better performance in both global and local structure. Li et al. also achieved significant results from the perspective of noisy image fusion using the low-rank representation [12].

With the development of deep learning, deep features are used as saliency features to fuse images. Liu et al. [19] suggested a convolutional sparse representation (CSR)-based image fusion. The CSR model was introduced by Zeiler et al. [28] in their deconvolutional networks for feature learning. Thus, although CSR is different from deep learning methods, the features extracted by CSR are still deep features. Liu et al. [18] also applied CNN model to image fusion, which can be used to generate the activity level measurement and fusion rule. Li et al. [13] proposed an effective image fusion method using the fixed VGG-19 [23] to generate a single image which contains all the features from infrared and visible images. But we all know that the training of deep model is very time consuming and complicated. And the requirements for hardware conditions are very high.

In this paper, we propose a novel and effective multifocus fusion method based on PCA filters of PCANet [4] which is a very simple deep learning model. The main contribution of this paper is using PCANet to extract image features and using nuclear norm to construct an effective feature space for image fusion. In particular, the training time of PCANet is shorter than that of other CNN-based network, and the extracted features can play the same role. The experimental results demonstrate that the proposed method can obtain state-of-the-art fusion performance in terms of both objective assessment and visual quality.

The structure of the rest paper is organized as follows. In Sect. 2, we give a brief introduction to related work. In Sect. 3, the proposed multi-focus image fusion method is presented in detail. Section 4 presents the experimental results. Finally, Sect. 5 concludes the paper and puts forward the future work.

2   Related Work

In [4], PCANet is a very simple deep learning network which contains three parts: cascaded principal component analysis (two-stage), binary hashing and block-wise histograms (output layer). In this architecture, PCA is employed to learn multistage filter banks. Therefore, this network can be designed and learned extremely easy and efficient. In this paper, we just use the PCA filters to extract image features, binary hashing and block-wise histograms are not used. In two-stage of PCANet [4], the number of filters in the first stage L1 is set as 8, the number of filters in the second stage L2 is the same. Therefore, we can get 8 image features in the first stage and 64 image features in the second stage. Considering the time efficiency and the non redundancy of the data, we just utilize image features of the first stage to fuse images. Therefore, the explanation of the first stage of PCANet is introduced as follows.

For each input image of size of $m \times n$, we take $k_1 \times k_2$ patches, and combine these patches (overlapping) together; i.e., $x_{i,1}, x_{i,2}, \cdots, x_{i,mn} \in R^{k_1 k_2}$, where $x_{i,j}$ denotes the $j - th$ vectorized patch in image I_i. Subtracting patch mean from each patch, we obtain $X_i = [\bar{x}_{i,1}, \bar{x}_{i,2}, \cdots, \bar{x}_{i,mn}]$, where $\bar{x}_{i,j}$ is a mean-centralized patch. Taking the same action for all input images $\{I_i\}_{i=1}^{N}$ (N is the number of the input images) and putting the results together, we get

$$X = [\bar{X}_1, \bar{X}_2, \cdots, \bar{X}_N] \in R^{K_1 K_2 \times N_{mn}} \tag{1}$$

Assuming that the number of filters in layer i is L_i, therefore, L_1, is the number of filters in layer 1. PCA minimizes the reconstruction error, i.e.,

$$\min_{V \in R^{K_1 K_2 \times L_1}} \|X - VV^T X\|_F^2, s.t. V^T V = I_{L_1} \tag{2}$$

where I_{L_1} is identity matrix of size $L_1 \times L_1$ and V is a matrix composed of eigenvectors corresponding to the first L_1 eigenvalues of X. Therefore, PCA filters is expressed as

$$W_l^1 = map_{k_1, k_2}(q_l(XX^T)) \in R^{K_1 K_2}, l = 1, 2, \cdots, L_1 \tag{3}$$

where $map_{k_1, k_2}(v)$ is a function that maps v to a matrix $W \in R^{K_1 K_2}$, and $q_l(XX^T)$ is the $l - th$ principal eigenvector of XX^T. The leading principal eigenvectors capture the main variations of all the mean-centralized training patches. Therefore we can use PCA filters to extract image features.

3   The Proposed Fusion Method

3.1   Image Features

Considering the generalization performance of the filters, we train the two-stage PCANet using ImageNet [22] which contains 1000 categories to get PCA filters. We randomly select 5 images for these 1000 categories, therefore, 5000 images in total are used to train PCA filters and all of them are resized to 256×256 and color images are converted to gray ones. Training PCA filters is implemented in Matlab R2016b on 3.60 GHz Inter(R) Core(TM) CPU with 64 GB RAM. We use the filters of the first stage to extract image features. For example, we use the fixed PCA filters to extract features from the source image, as shown in Fig. 1.

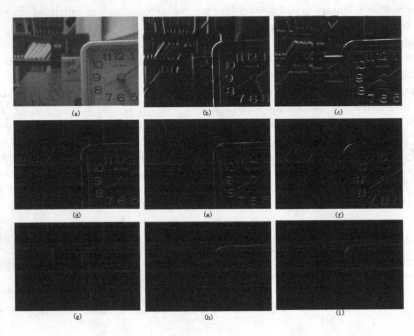

Fig. 1. (a) is an original image and (b)–(i) are image features obtained by the PCA filters of the first stage of the PCANet.

In Fig. 1, (a) is a near focused source image. (b)–(i) are image features extracted by PCA filters, such as texture features, vertical textures, horizontal textures, point textures, diagonal textures, etc. Obviously, the first few images extract features from a global perspective, and the subsequent features become more specific to local significance. Image fusion is the fusion of images with different contents of the same scene into an image. In other words, the saliency features of different images are extracted and combined into an image. In [3], to get better performance, the authors remove the first three principal components in the Eigenface method. Therefore, the feature extraction before fusion can reflect the significance of the source image as much as possible. Because of that, we do an experiment in which there are four cases including all the 8 image features or discarding the first image feature or discarding second one or both of them are abandoned.

Experimental results show that it is better to discard the first two feature maps. Therefore we just utilize the last six feature maps to make the activity level map. This experiment will be introduced in detail in Sect. 4.2.

3.2 Proposed Fusion Method

In this section we will introduce the proposed fusion method in detail. The framework of the proposed fusion method is shown in Fig. 2.

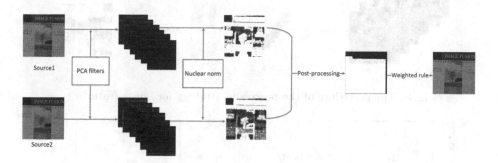

Fig. 2. The framework of the proposed method.

As shown in Fig. 2, the input images are denoted by $Source_1$ and $Source_2$ respectively the feature extraction of the $Source_1$ and $Source_2$ is carried out through the pre-trained PCA filters. We just take the last six image features to calculate the activity level map.

In the [11], authors apply the nuclear norm to the image features. In this paper, we use nuclear norm [17] which is the sum of the singular values of matrix to extract the image features to get the activity level maps. This procedure is shown in Fig. 3.

As shown in Fig. 3, the edge of the feature map is filled with zero, the six feature maps are concatenated as a 6-channel image feature, and the multi-channel image feature is processed by nuclear norm. Taking each pixel as the center, multi-channel block is taken from the same position, and the multi-channel block is transformed into a two-dimensional matrix. The sum of the singular values of the matrix is calculated, and the sum value is used to replace the original pixel point. Therefore, activity level maps are composed of the sum of singular values.

$$M_k(x,y) = ||R(F_k^{1:c}[(x-t):(x+t),(y-t):(y+t)])||_*, \qquad (4)$$
$$c = 6, k \in \{1,2\}, t = 2$$

where $R(*)$ is reshape operation, (x,y) is the position of the pixel, c is channel number, k is the number of preregistered source image, $(2t+1) \times (2t+1)$ is the block size, $M_k(*)$ is the activity level map and $F_k^{1:c}(*)$ is c feature maps of the $k-th$ source image.

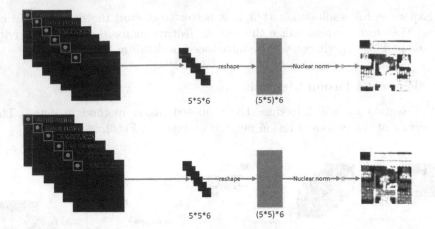

Fig. 3. The procedure of the processing strategy for image features.

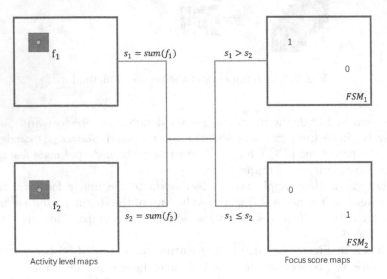

Fig. 4. The construction of focus score maps through the silding window technique.

Next, the activity level map is processed to obtain the decision map. According to the reference [21], we process the activity level maps as shown in Fig. 4.

In Fig. 4, for each corresponding pair of blocks which take each pixel as the center f_1 and f_2, we calculate the sum of all the coefficients in each of them, denoted as s_1 and s_2. If $s_1 > s_2$, the corresponding pixel is set as 1, otherwise, the pixel is set as 0. Finally, we can obtain two complementary focus score maps, denoted as FSM_1 and FSM_2. The steps are shown in Eqs. 5 and 6.

$$FSM_k(x, y) = \begin{cases} 1 & \text{if } s_k > s_n \\ 0 & \text{if } s_k \leq s_n \end{cases}, k \in \{1, 2\}, n \in \{1, 2\}, k \neq n \tag{5}$$

$$s_i = sum(f_i), i \in \{1, 2\} \tag{6}$$

where $sum(*)$ is the sum of all coefficients in f_i.

As focus score maps usually contain some small holes surrounded by the focused regions, we apply a simple post-processing approach to remove these regions. We apply a small region removal strategy [18] that the area threshold is universally set to $0.1 \times H \times W$, where H and W are the height and width of each source image. Subsequently, we apply morphological closing and opening operation to the focus score maps. Finally, according to [21], we combine the two focus score maps into one decision map, that is, for the pixels where the two focus score maps are complementary, take the value of the first focus score map; otherwise, the value is 0.5. The final decision map denoted as D_{final} is evaluated as shown in formula 7.

$$D_{final} = \begin{cases} FSM_1(x,y) & FSM_1(x,y) \neq FSM_2(x,y) \\ 0.5 & FSM_1(x,y) = FSM_2(x,y) \end{cases} \tag{7}$$

Finally, we obtain the D_{final} shown in Fig. 5 (a).

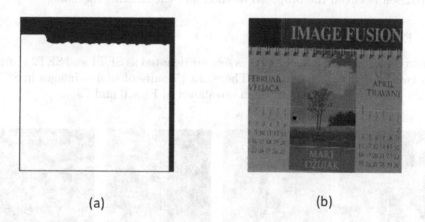

(a)   (b)

Fig. 5. (a) is D_{final} and (b) is fused image.

3.3   Fusion Method

With the final decision map D_{final}, the fused image F is calculated by

$$F = D_{final}Source_1 + (1 - D_{final})Source_2. \tag{8}$$

The fused image is shown in Fig. 5(b).
The algorithm is described in Table 1.

Table 1. Algorithm flow chart

(Input): Two registered source images
(Output): The fused image
(1) Training the two stages of PCANet on ImageNet to get PCA filters which are used to extract image features
(2) Applying the nuclear norm to image features, the activity level maps are obtained by Eq. 4
(3) According to Eqs. 5 and 6, the focus score maps are obtained by the activity level maps. Then, applying a simple post-processing approach and Eq. 7 to get the final decision map
(4) Finally, the fused image is obtained by Eq. 8

4   Experiments

In this section, we introduce the source images and experimental environment. There is also a detailed description of Sect. 3.1 and a subjective and objective comparison between the proposed method and the existing methods.

4.1   Experimental Settings

As introduced in Sect. 3.1, our images sets are denoted as SET1 and SET2 coming from two references [29] and [10]. There are 15 pairs of source images in SET1 and 20 pairs in SET2. Part of them are shown in Figs. 6 and 7.

Fig. 6. Four pairs of source images from SET1.

Secondly, we compare the proposed method with several existing fusion methods, including: convolutional sparse representation fusion method (CSR) [19],

Fig. 7. Four pairs of source images from SET2.

multi-focus image fusion with dense SIFT (DSIFT) [21], multi-focus image fusion with a deep convolutional neural network (CNN) [18], infrared and visible image fusion using a deep learning framework (VGG) [13], discrete cosine harmonic wavelet transform fusion method (DCHWT) [7] and cross bilateral filter fusion method (CBF) [8].

In order to evaluate our proposed method and existing methods from an objective perspective, we choose several image quality metrics. These are: Average Gradient (AG), entropy(EN), Mutual Information (MI) [1], FMI_gradient [6] and the sum of the correlations of differences (SCD) [2].

In our experiment, the sliding window size is 5×5 in nuclear norm used for feature processing and the step is one pixel. The sliding window size is 3×3 in the construction of focus score maps and the step is one pixel as well.

The fusion algorithm is implemented in Matlab R2016a on 3.00 GHz Inter(R) Core(TM) CPU with 4 GB RAM.

4.2   Feature Selection Experiment

In this section, we will introduce the experiment which is mentioned in Sect. 3.1. In this two images sets (SET1 and SET2), according to the number of image features, our method is divided into four cases: (1) all features are used, (2) discarding the first image feature, (3) discarding the second image feature and (4) discarding the first two image features. For all the cases, we compare each other and adopt multiple evaluation indexes as reference, and take the average value of experimental results of each image as the final, as shown in Tables 2 and 3.

In Tables 2 and 3, the best results are bloded. It can be seen from the two tables that the distribution of the best results is the same in the four cases of each data set, but the value of the fourth case is better than or equal to the first three cases. Therefore, only the last six image features are selected, and the first two are abandoned.

Table 2. The AG, EN, MI and FMI_gradient average values of the compared methods and the proposed method for SET1.

SET1	(1)	(2)	(3)	(4)
AG	0.0995	0.0995	0.0999	**0.1001**
EN	7.2779	7.2766	7.2782	**7.2787**
MI	14.5558	14.5531	14.5565	**14.5575**
FMI_gradient	0.6634	0.6656	0.6625	**0.6646**

Table 3. The AG, EN, MI and SCD average values of the compared methods and the proposed method for SET2.

SET2	(1)	(2)	(3)	(4)
AG	0.1083	0.1083	**0.1083**	0.1083
EN	7.4127	7.4128	**7.4132**	7.4132
MI	14.8254	14.8256	**14.8263**	14.8263
FMI_gradient	0.4726	0.4727	**0.4728**	0.4728

4.3   Image Fusion Results

We use fifteen pairs of source images (SET1) to test comparison methods and the proposed method. The fused results are shown in Fig. 8, we choose one pair of source images as an example. And the values of AG, EN, MI and FMI_gradient for fifteen fused images are shown in Tables 4 and 5.

As shown in Fig. 8, we can see, the proposed method has almost the same fusion performance compared with other classical and novel fusion methods in human visual system. Therefore we mainly discus the fusion performance with quality metrics, as shown in Tables 4 and 5.

In Tables 4 and 5, the best results are bloded, the second-best results are marked in red. We can see, in most cases, the proposed method has good indicators.

We also make the same comparison on SET2 which contains 20 pairs of source images. The fused results are shown in Fig. 9, we choose one pair of source images as an example as well. And the values of AG, EN, MI and SCD for twenty fused images are shown in Tables 6 and 7.

As shown in Fig. 9, we can see, from human visual perspective, there is almost no significant difference in the fusion results between these methods. Therefore we evaluate the fusion results objectively, as shown in Tables 6 and 7.

In Tables 6 and 7, the best results are bloded, the second-best results are marked in red. We can see, in most cases, the proposed method has good indicators as well.

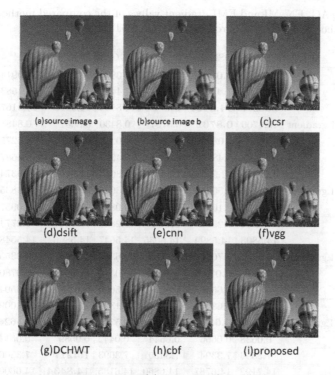

Fig. 8. The examples of fused results. (a) Source image a; (b) Source image b; (c) csr; (d) dsift; (e) cnn; (f) vgg; (g) DCHWT; (h) cbf; (i) The proposed method.

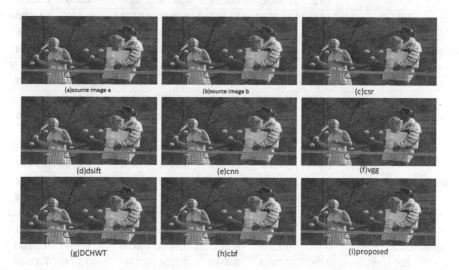

Fig. 9. The examples of fused results. (a) Source image a; (b) Source image b; (c) csr; (d) dsift; (e) cnn; (f) vgg; (g) DCHWT; (h) cbf; (i) The proposed method.

Table 4. The AG, EN, MI and FMI_gradient values of the compared methods and the proposed method for 10 pairs source images from SET1.

SET1		CSR	DSIFT	CNN	VGG	DCHWT	CBF	OURS
image1	AG	0.0957	**0.0985**	**0.0985**	0.0805	0.0934	0.0914	0.0982
	EN	7.4689	**7.4712**	7.4711	7.4447	7.4585	7.4583	7.4709
	MI	14.9377	**14.9424**	14.9422	14.8895	14.9170	14.9167	14.9419
	FMI_gradient	0.4700	**0.8761**	0.8757	0.8430	0.8001	0.8488	0.8738
image2	AG	0.0302	0.0308	0.0308	0.0216	0.0277	0.0275	**0.0309**
	EN	6.4619	6.4814	6.4788	6.4307	6.4734	6.4687	**6.4826**
	MI	12.9238	12.9628	12.9575	12.8615	12.9468	12.9374	**12.9652**
	FMI_gradient	0.2548	0.5554	0.5358	0.3678	0.3464	0.3835	**0.5683**
image3	AG	0.1030	0.1043	0.1059	0.0830	0.0994	0.0957	**0.1063**
	EN	7.2904	7.2950	**7.3017**	7.2823	7.2933	7.2774	7.3012
	MI	14.5808	14.5899	14.6035	14.5647	14.5866	14.5548	**14.6025**
	FMI_gradient	0.5254	0.7039	**0.7068**	0.6359	0.5960	0.6355	0.7065
image4	AG	0.0816	**0.0847**	0.0830	0.0538	0.0804	0.0780	0.0846
	EN	6.6060	6.6587	6.6534	6.5660	**6.6780**	6.6504	6.6571
	MI	13.2120	13.3174	13.3068	13.1321	**13.3560**	13.3009	13.3142
	FMI_gradient	0.4966	**0.6379**	0.6348	0.5315	0.4561	0.5624	0.6350
image5	AG	0.0638	0.0656	0.0644	0.0442	0.0589	0.0614	**0.0674**
	EN	7.3596	7.3394	7.3430	7.3093	**7.4217**	7.3300	7.3324
	MI	14.7192	14.6787	14.6860	14.6185	**14.8434**	14.6600	14.6648
	FMI_gradient	0.4603	0.6355	0.6294	0.5278	0.4359	0.5324	**0.6424**
image6	AG	0.0841	**0.0865**	**0.0865**	0.0616	0.0806	0.0766	**0.0865**
	EN	7.4277	7.4376	7.4329	7.3518	7.3876	7.3755	**7.4398**
	MI	14.8554	14.8753	14.8658	14.7036	14.7751	14.7509	**14.8796**
	FMI_gradient	0.4674	0.6220	0.6130	0.5232	0.4817	0.5214	**0.6288**
image7	AG	0.0863	0.0886	0.0881	0.0584	0.0828	0.0810	**0.0888**
	EN	7.2580	7.2547	7.2560	7.1865	**7.2582**	7.2496	7.2538
	MI	14.5160	14.5095	14.5120	14.3731	**14.5165**	14.4992	14.5077
	FMI_gradient	0.4735	**0.6185**	0.6168	0.5181	0.4543	0.5143	0.6183
image8	AG	0.1001	0.1034	0.1025	0.0823	0.0952	0.0922	**0.1036**
	EN	7.1272	**7.1448**	7.1421	7.1041	7.1199	7.1133	7.1445
	MI	14.2544	**14.2895**	14.2842	14.2082	14.2397	14.2266	14.2891
	FMI_gradient	0.6411	0.7085	0.7120	0.6778	0.6451	0.6702	**0.7123**
image9	AG	0.1066	0.1066	0.1102	0.0860	0.1018	0.0966	**0.1114**
	EN	7.8323	7.8322	7.8376	7.8287	7.8366	7.8351	**7.8402**
	MI	15.6645	15.6643	15.6751	15.6574	15.6733	15.6701	**15.6803**
	FMI_gradient	0.6611	0.6925	0.6955	0.6615	0.6406	0.6622	**0.6941**
image10	AG	0.1107	0.1155	0.1133	0.0718	0.1058	0.1041	**0.1160**
	EN	7.7827	7.7933	7.7870	7.7251	7.7747	7.7747	**7.7946**
	MI	15.5655	15.5866	15.5741	15.4502	15.5494	15.5494	**15.5893**
	FMI_gradient	0.5423	0.5972	0.5965	0.4940	0.4871	0.5248	**0.5983**

Table 5. The AG, EN, MI and FMI_gradient values of the compared methods and the proposed method for another 5 pairs source images from SET1.

SET1		CSR	DSIFT	CNN	VGG	DCHWT	CBF	OURS
image11	AG	0.0728	0.0750	0.0747	0.0511	0.0693	0.0694	**0.0753**
	EN	7.0322	7.0689	7.0222	6.9620	7.0523	**7.0690**	7.0245
	MI	14.0644	14.1377	14.0443	13.9240	14.1047	**14.1379**	14.0491
	FMI_gradient	0.4372	0.5947	**0.6411**	0.5459	0.4384	0.4996	0.6282
image12	AG	0.0876	0.0906	0.0887	0.0561	0.0818	0.0863	**0.0908**
	EN	7.3282	7.3379	7.3295	7.2406	7.3064	7.3195	**7.3404**
	MI	14.6565	14.6758	14.6589	14.4811	14.6127	14.6391	**14.6809**
	FMI_gradient	0.5249	0.6159	0.6122	0.5273	0.4943	0.5375	**0.6165**
image13	AG	0.0967	**0.1001**	0.0997	0.0762	0.0929	0.0954	0.1000
	EN	7.3415	7.3738	7.3740	7.3687	**7.3879**	7.3705	7.3741
	MI	14.6830	14.7475	14.7479	14.7375	**14.7758**	14.7411	14.7483
	FMI_gradient	0.6839	0.8539	**0.8547**	0.8322	0.7497	0.8369	0.8537
image14	AG	0.1780	0.1853	0.1830	0.1000	0.1647	0.1626	**0.1860**
	EN	7.2781	7.3062	7.2926	6.9421	7.1410	7.1515	**7.3102**
	MI	14.5561	14.6124	14.5852	13.8841	14.2819	14.3030	**14.6204**
	FMI_gradient	0.5753	**0.6085**	0.6000	0.4231	0.4283	0.4798	0.5961
image15	AG	0.1514	**0.1557**	0.1540	0.1014	0.1364	0.1405	0.1554
	EN	7.5571	7.4203	7.4427	7.5480	**7.7075**	7.5827	7.4144
	MI	15.1142	14.8407	14.8854	15.0960	**15.4149**	15.1654	14.8289
	FMI_gradient	0.5039	0.5899	0.5847	0.4870	0.4180	0.5044	**0.5972**

Table 6. The AG, EN, MI and SCD values of the compared methods and the proposed method for 10 pairs source images from SET2.

SET2		CSR	DSIFT	CNN	VGG	DCHWT	CBF	OURS
image1	AG	0.0610	0.0620	0.0619	0.0511	0.0581	0.0566	**0.0629**
	EN	6.8647	6.8664	6.8666	6.8466	6.8634	6.8757	**6.8813**
	MI	13.7294	13.7329	13.7333	13.6932	13.7269	13.7515	**13.7625**
	SCD	0.3889	0.3904	0.4100	0.1841	0.3089	0.3125	**0.4547**
image2	AG	0.1027	0.1068	0.1059	0.0766	0.1004	0.0967	**0.1072**
	EN	7.5038	**7.5141**	7.5124	7.4793	7.5054	7.4957	7.5101
	MI	15.0075	**15.0281**	15.0248	14.9586	15.0108	14.9915	15.0202
	SCD	0.4366	**0.4905**	0.4874	0.2553	0.3523	0.3579	0.4678

Table 6. (*continued*)

SET2		CSR	DSIFT	CNN	VGG	DCHWT	CBF	OURS
image3	AG	0.0935	0.0964	0.0956	0.0717	0.0910	0.0842	**0.0968**
	EN	7.5205	**7.5364**	7.5349	7.5020	7.5246	7.5151	7.5353
	MI	15.0410	**15.0727**	15.0698	15.0040	15.0493	15.0301	15.0706
	SCD	0.4293	**0.4772**	0.4724	0.2408	0.3511	0.3021	0.4690
image4	AG	0.1004	0.1047	0.1031	0.0749	0.0984	0.0912	**0.1052**
	EN	7.5335	7.5542	7.5519	7.4801	7.5406	7.5263	**7.5589**
	MI	15.0669	15.1083	15.1037	14.9602	15.0812	15.0527	**15.1178**
	SCD	0.4219	0.4560	0.4506	0.2456	0.3571	0.3238	**0.4549**
image5	AG	0.0901	0.0925	0.0920	0.0744	0.0862	0.0819	**0.0932**
	EN	7.6695	7.6756	7.6746	7.6517	7.6625	7.6558	**7.6786**
	MI	15.3390	15.3512	15.3491	15.3033	15.3251	15.3116	**15.3571**
	SCD	0.4387	0.4799	0.4751	0.2102	0.3346	0.2636	**0.5088**
image6	AG	0.0841	0.0859	0.0841	0.0625	0.0818	0.0746	**0.0866**
	EN	7.0884	7.1263	7.1241	7.0883	**7.1538**	7.1222	7.1340
	MI	14.1768	14.2525	14.2482	14.1766	**14.3077**	14.2444	14.2681
	SCD	0.2906	0.3302	0.3242	0.1949	0.2628	0.2270	**0.3384**
image7	AG	0.0746	0.0764	0.0762	0.0557	0.0729	0.0674	**0.0773**
	EN	7.2883	7.3089	7.3078	7.2659	7.3073	7.3024	**7.3154**
	MI	14.5767	14.6179	14.6156	14.5318	14.6146	14.6047	**14.6309**
	SCD	0.2584	**0.3168**	0.3158	0.1857	0.2257	0.1927	0.3129
image8	AG	0.1696	0.1745	0.1726	0.1140	0.1653	0.1560	**0.1746**
	EN	7.4343	7.4531	7.4498	7.3585	7.4415	7.4157	**7.4554**
	MI	14.8686	14.9063	14.8997	14.7171	14.8830	14.8314	**14.9109**
	SCD	0.6795	**0.6972**	0.6933	0.4368	0.6029	0.6116	**0.6972**
image9	AG	0.1495	0.1543	0.1530	0.1034	0.1459	0.1378	**0.1550**
	EN	7.6738	**7.6883**	7.6870	7.6179	7.6707	7.6535	7.6855
	MI	15.3475	**15.3767**	15.3739	15.2358	15.3415	15.3070	15.3710
	SCD	0.5786	**0.6140**	0.6088	0.3674	0.4962	0.4928	0.5813
image10	AG	0.1150	0.1183	0.1176	0.0875	0.1115	0.1030	**0.1185**
	EN	7.4619	7.4853	7.4830	7.4326	**7.4903**	7.4785	7.4884
	MI	14.9239	14.9705	14.9660	14.8652	**14.9806**	14.9570	14.9767
	SCD	0.4442	**0.4912**	0.4881	0.2396	0.3422	0.2873	0.4888

Table 7. The AG, EN, MI and SCD values of the compared methods and the proposed method for another 10 pairs source images from SET2.

SET2		CSR	DSIFT	CNN	VGG	DCHWT	CBF	OURS
image11	AG	0.0648	0.0659	0.0655	0.0514	0.0633	0.0564	**0.0668**
	EN	7.0320	7.0404	7.0403	7.0350	**7.0517**	7.0474	7.0494
	MI	14.0641	14.0808	14.0805	14.0700	14.1033	14.0949	**14.0988**
	SCD	0.2500	0.2893	0.2872	0.1565	0.2039	0.1383	**0.3036**
image12	AG	0.0974	0.1021	0.1013	0.0704	0.0961	0.0929	**0.1025**
	EN	7.0401	7.0711	7.0645	6.9295	7.0319	7.0393	**7.0748**
	MI	14.0802	14.1423	14.1290	13.8590	14.0637	14.0786	**14.1497**
	SCD	0.5151	0.5549	0.5428	0.3314	0.4740	0.5025	**0.5680**
image13	AG	0.0987	0.1004	0.0998	0.0732	0.0964	0.0877	**0.1014**
	EN	7.3394	7.3571	7.3556	7.2960	7.3530	7.3302	**7.3625**
	MI	14.6787	14.7143	14.7112	14.5920	14.7060	14.6604	**14.7249**
	SCD	0.3363	**0.3954**	0.3924	0.2185	0.2910	0.2449	0.3896
image14	AG	0.0759	0.0785	0.0783	0.0606	0.0750	0.0694	**0.0795**
	EN	7.5955	7.6102	7.6092	7.5695	7.5959	7.5907	**7.6135**
	MI	15.1910	15.2205	15.2185	15.1390	15.1919	15.1814	**15.2271**
	SCD	0.3024	**0.3691**	0.3654	0.1918	0.2647	0.2125	0.3563
image15	AG	0.1042	0.1055	0.1048	0.0809	0.1005	0.0935	**0.1069**
	EN	7.4169	7.4124	7.4136	7.4118	**7.4299**	7.4162	7.4172
	MI	14.8339	14.8247	14.8273	14.8237	**14.8598**	14.8325	14.8345
	SCD	0.5054	0.5398	0.5271	0.2756	0.3836	0.3345	**0.5414**
image16	AG	0.1145	**0.1184**	0.1167	0.0847	0.1119	0.1020	0.1182
	EN	7.1316	7.1596	7.1567	7.0791	7.1452	7.1368	**7.1655**
	MI	14.2631	14.3193	14.3135	14.1582	14.2903	14.2736	**14.3311**
	SCD	0.4453	0.4715	0.4653	0.2518	0.3731	0.3083	**0.4888**
image17	AG	0.1594	0.1647	0.1629	0.1113	0.1561	0.1437	**0.1649**
	EN	7.7790	**7.7817**	7.7819	7.7329	7.7720	7.7647	7.7796
	MI	15.5579	15.5634	15.5638	15.4657	15.5439	15.5293	**15.5593**
	SCD	0.5938	**0.6160**	0.6082	0.3571	0.4972	0.4140	0.5970
image18	AG	0.1432	0.1487	0.1475	0.0994	0.1408	0.1344	**0.1493**
	EN	7.4088	7.4331	7.4294	7.2854	7.3958	7.3940	**7.4385**
	MI	14.8176	14.8662	14.8588	14.5707	14.7915	14.7881	**14.8770**
	SCD	0.6146	**0.6398**	0.6353	0.3933	0.5504	0.5599	0.6375
image19	AG	0.1061	0.1123	0.1111	0.0717	0.1077	0.1030	**0.1125**
	EN	7.4622	7.4888	7.4841	7.3596	7.4674	7.4627	**7.4922**
	MI	14.9245	14.9775	14.9682	14.7193	14.9349	14.9253	**14.9844**
	SCD	0.4075	0.4311	0.4283	0.2667	0.3727	0.3592	**0.4323**
image20	AG	0.0840	0.0854	0.0852	0.0615	0.0810	0.0759	**0.0860**
	EN	7.6188	7.6243	7.6239	7.5925	7.6142	7.6128	**7.6271**
	MI	15.2377	15.2486	15.2478	15.1850	15.2284	15.2255	**15.2542**
	SCD	0.2762	0.3566	0.3338	0.2151	0.2503	0.2719	**0.3670**

5 Conclusion

In this paper, we propose a novel fusion method based on PCANet. First of all, we utilize the PCA filters to extract image features of source images, and then we apply the nuclear norm to process the image features in order to get activity level maps. Through a series of post-processing operations on activity level maps, the decision map is obtained. Finally, the fused image is obtained by utilizing a weighted fusion rule. The experimental results demonstrate that the proposed method can obtain state-of-the-art fusion performance in terms of both objective assessment and visual quality.

References

1. Mutual information. https://ww2.mathworks.cn/matlabcentral/fileexchange/28694-mutual-information
2. Aslantas, V., Bendes, E.: A new image quality metric for image fusion: the sum of the correlations of differences. AEU Int. J. Electron. Commun. **69**(12), 1890–1896 (2015)
3. Belhumeur, P.N., Hespanha, J.P., Kriegman, D.J.: Eigenfaces vs. fisherfaces: recognition using class specific linear projection. Technical report, Yale University New Haven United States (1997)
4. Chan, T.-H., Jia, K., Gao, S., Jiwen, L., Zeng, Z., Ma, Y.: PCANet: a simple deep learning baseline for image classification? IEEE Trans. Image Process. **24**(12), 5017–5032 (2015)
5. Guo, L., Dai, M., Zhu, M.: Multifocus color image fusion based on quaternion curvelet transform. Opt. Express **20**(17), 18846–18860 (2012)
6. Haghighat, M., Razian,M.A.: Fast-FMI: non-reference image fusion metric. In: 2014 IEEE 8th International Conference on Application of Information and Communication Technologies (AICT), pp. 1–3. IEEE (2014)
7. Shreyamsha Kumar, B.K.: Multifocus and multispectral image fusion based on pixel significance using discrete cosine harmonic wavelet transform. Signal Image Video Process. **7**(6), 1125–1143 (2013)
8. Shreyamsha Kumar, B.K.: Image fusion based on pixel significance using cross bilateral filter. Signal Image Video Process. **9**(5), 1193–1204 (2015)
9. Li, H., Manjunath, B.S., Mitra, S.K.: Multisensor image fusion using the wavelet transform. Graph. Models Image Process. **57**(3), 235–245 (1995)
10. Li, H., Wu, X.-J.: Multi-focus Image fusion using dictionary learning and low-rank representation. In: Zhao, Y., Kong, X., Taubman, D. (eds.) ICIG 2017. LNCS, vol. 10666, pp. 675–686. Springer, Cham (2017). https://doi.org/10.1007/978-3-319-71607-7_59
11. Li, H., Wu,X.-J.: Infrared and visible image fusion with ResNet and zero-phase component analysis. arXiv preprint arXiv:1806.07119 (2018)
12. Li,H., Wu, X.-J.: Multi-focus noisy image fusion using low-rank representation. arXiv preprint arXiv:1804.09325 (2018)
13. Li, H., Wu, X.-J., Kittler,J.: Infrared and visible image fusion using a deep learning framework. arXiv preprint arXiv:1804.06992 (2018)
14. Li, S., Kang, X., Fang, L., Jianwen, H., Yin, H.: Pixel-level image fusion: a survey of the state of the art. Inf. Fusion **33**, 100–112 (2017)

15. Li, S., Kang, X., Jianwen, H., Yang, B.: Image matting for fusion of multi-focus images in dynamic scenes. Inf. Fusion **14**(2), 147–162 (2013)
16. Liu, C.H., Qi, Y., Ding, W.R.: Infrared and visible image fusion method based on saliency detection in sparse domain. Infrared Phys. Technol. **83**, 94–102 (2017)
17. Liu, G., Lin, Z., Yu, Y.: Robust subspace segmentation by low-rank representation. In: Proceedings of the 27th International Conference on Machine Learning (ICML-2010), pp. 663–670 (2010)
18. Liu, Y., Chen, X., Peng, H., Wang, Z.: Multi-focus image fusion with a deep convolutional neural network. Inf. Fusion **36**, 191–207 (2017)
19. Liu, Y., Chen, X., Ward, R.K., Wang, Z.J.: Image fusion with convolutional sparse representation. IEEE Signal Process. Lett. **23**(12), 1882–1886 (2016)
20. Liu, Y., Liu, S., Wang, Z.: A general framework for image fusion based on multi-scale transform and sparse representation. Inf. Fusion **24**, 147–164 (2015)
21. Liu, Y., Liu, S., Wang, Z.: Multi-focus image fusion with dense sift. Inf. Fusion **23**, 139–155 (2015)
22. Russakovsky, O., et al.: Imagenet large scale visual recognition challenge. Int. J. Comput. Vis. **115**(3), 211–252 (2015)
23. Simonyan, K., Zisserman, A.: Very deep convolutional networks for large-scale image recognition. arXiv preprint arXiv:1409.1556 (2014)
24. Wang, L., Li, B., Tian, L.-F.: EGGDD: an explicit dependency model for multi-modal medical image fusion in shift-invariant shearlet transform domain. Inf. Fusion **19**, 29–37 (2014)
25. Yang, S., Wang, M., Jiao, L., Wu, R., Wang, Z.: Image fusion based on a new contourlet packet. Inf. Fusion **11**(2), 78–84 (2010)
26. Yang, Y., Yang, M., Huang, S., Ding, M., Sun, J.: Robust sparse representation combined with adaptive PCNN for multifocus image fusion. IEEE Access **6**, 20138–20151 (2018)
27. Yin, H., Li, Y., Chai, Y., Liu, Z., Zhu, Z.: A novel sparse-representation-based multi-focus image fusion approach. Neurocomputing **216**, 216–229 (2016)
28. Zeiler, M.D., Krishnan, D., Taylor, G.W., Fergus, R.: Deconvolutional networks (2010)
29. Zhang, Y., Bai, X., Wang, T.: Boundary finding based multi-focus image fusion through multi-scale morphological focus-measure. Inf. fusion **35**, 81–101 (2017)

An Image Captioning Method for Infant Sleeping Environment Diagnosis

Xinyi Liu[1(✉)] and Mariofanna Milanova[2]

[1] System Engineering Department, University of Arkansas at Little Rock,
Little Rock, USA
xxliu8@ualr.edu
[2] Computer Science Department, University of Arkansas at Little Rock,
Little Rock, USA
mgmilanova@ualr.edu

Abstract. This paper presents a new method of image captioning, which generate textual description of an image. We applied our method for infant sleeping environment analysis and diagnosis to describe the image with the infant sleeping position, sleeping surface and bedding condition, which involves recognition and representation of body pose, activity and surrounding environment. In this challenging case, visual attention as an essential part of human visual perception is employed to efficiently process the visual input. Texture analysis is used to give a precise diagnosis of sleeping surface. The encoder-decoder model was trained by Microsoft COCO dataset combined with our own annotated dataset contains relevant information. The result shows it is able to generate description of the image and address the potential risk factors in the image, then give the corresponding advice based on the generated caption. It proved its ability to assist human in infant care-giving area and potential in other human assistive systems.

Keywords: Image captioning · Visual attention · Assistive systems

1 Introduction

Sudden Infant Death Syndrome (SIDS) [1] has been a leading cause of death among babies younger than 1 year old. It is the sudden, unexplained death that even after a complete investigation [2], still hard to find a cause of the death. Although the exact cause of SIDS is still unknown, we can reduce the risk of SIDS and other Sleep-related causes of infant death by providing a safe infant sleeping environment.

Previous research was mostly about monitoring motion or physical condition of infants, but to the best of our knowledge there is no application for Sleep environment diagnosis yet. And considering the advice from American Academy of Pediatrics (AAP) [7] to reduce risk of SIDS is through provide a safe infant sleeping environment.

In our opinion, Sleep environment diagnosis is needed, to help parents or caregivers aware of risk factors and realize what can be improved. To this end, we proposed a system to help generate the analysis of infant sleeping position and sleeping

F. Schwenker and S. Scherer (Eds.): MPRSS 2018, LNAI 11377, pp. 18–26, 2019.
https://doi.org/10.1007/978-3-030-20984-1_2

environment. Given a photograph of the infant sleeping or just the sleeping environment, it can generate natural-language description of the analysis.

It is a process used both natural language processing and computer vision to generate textual description of an image. And can be viewed as a challenging task in scene understanding, as it not only need to express the local information as object recognition task do, it also need to show higher level of information, the relationship of local information. There has been a significant progress made in Image captioning recent years, with development of Deep Learning (CNN and LSTM) and large-scale datasets. Instead of performing object detection and organizing words in sequence, several encoder-decoder frameworks [3–5] used deep neural network trained end-to-end.

Visual Attention [6] is an essential part of human visual perception, it also plays an important role in understanding a visual scene by efficiently locate region of interest and analyze the scene by selectively processing subsets of visual input. This is especially important when the scene is cluttered with multiple elements, by dynamically process salient features it can help us better understand primary information of the scene.

In this paper, we describe the approach of generating the analysis of the infant sleeping environment, which incorporated visual attention model to efficiently to narrow down the search and speed up the process. Different from other image captioning task, which usually just aimed to give a general description of the scene, we also need more detailed information regarding to certain area of interest. In our case, the bedding condition is essential for the analysis, we extracted image's texture feature to conduct analysis.

The contributions of this paper are the following: We introduced a new framework of image captioning in special case to help diagnosis and analysis the infant sleeping environment, both low and high level of visual information were used to give a caption that not only shows the relation of visual elements, but also give the detailed information of the certain area of interest. We validated our method on the real-world data, which shows the satisfactory performance.

2 Related Work

2.1 Image Captioning

Recently, image captioning has been a field of interest for researchers in both academia and industry [10–12]. Some classic models are mainly template-based [24–26] methods, combine detected words from visual input and sentence fragments to generate the sentence using pre-defined templates. These methods are limited in generating variety of words, could not achieve a satisfactory performance. With the development of deep learning and inspired by the sequence to sequence training with neural network used in machine translation problem, Karpathy et al. [11] proposed to align sentence snippets to the visual regions by computing a visual-semantic similarity score. Vinyals et al. [13] used LSTM [18] RNNs for their model. They used CNN to encode image then passed to LSTM to encode sentences.

2.2 Visual Attention

The visual attention models are mainly categorized into Bottom-up models and top-down models [6]. Bottom-up attention models are based on the image feature of the visual scene. Such as histogram-based contrast (HC) and region-based contrast (RC) algorithm proposed in [15]. Top-down attention models are driven by the observer's prior knowledge and current goal. Minh et al. proposed recurrent attention model (RAM) [16] to mimic human attention and eye movement mechanism, to predict future eye movements and location to see at next time step. Based on RAM, recurrent visual attention model (DRAM) [17] was proposed to expand it for multiple object recognition by exploring the image in a sequential manner with attention mechanism, then generate a label sequence for multiple objects. Xu et al. [14] introduced an attention-based model to generate neural image caption, a generative LSTM can focus on different attention regions of the visual input while generating the corresponding caption. It has two variants: stochastic "hard" attention, trained by maximizing a variational lower bound through the reinforcement learning, and deterministic "soft" attention, trained using standard back-propagation techniques.

3 Background and Requirement

American Academy of Pediatrics (AAP) Task Force on SIDS recommend place infant in a supine position, [7] let them wholly sleep on their back until 1 year of age. Research shows that the back-sleeping position carries the lowest risk of SIDS. Side sleeping is nor safe and not advised.

And it's necessary to use a firm sleep surface covered by a fitted sheet without other bedding and soft objects, keep soft objects such as pillow or comforters and loose bedding such as blanket away from the sleep area.

It also recommended that infants should share the bedroom, but sleep on a separate surface designed for baby. Room-sharing but no bed-sharing removes the possibility of suffocation, strangulation, and entrapment that may occur when the infant is sleeping in the adult bed.

In the past, there had been a lot of research or devices developed for safety of infant, such as smart baby monitor [8], equipped with camera, microphone and motion sensor, so that parents can stream on their mobile devices and get to know the baby's sleeping patterns. Home apnea monitor were also used for similar purposes [9], monitoring infant's heart rate and oxygen level.

Although these seems helpful and make monitoring infant easier, AAP still advised not to use home cardiorespiratory monitors as a strategy to reduce the risk of SIDS, as it hasn't shown scientific evidence to decrease the incidence of SIDS.

In short, in this case, we should analyze the infant sleeping position, bedding condition and soft objects to help diagnose the infant sleeping environment.

4 Approach

In this section, we describe our algorithm and the proposed architecture (Fig. 1).

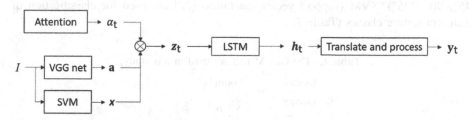

Fig. 1. Architecture of the model, (α_t: attention vector, a: annotation vector, x: texture vector. z_t: context vector, h_t: hidden state, y_t: generated sentence)

4.1 Encoder

We first encode input image I to a sequence of words. Normalize the input image to size of 224 × 224. VGG net [22] was used to generate D-dimensional annotation vectors a_i, which describe different local region of the image. Without losing detailed local information, features by 14 × 14 × 512 dimension from Conv5_3 layer was used here.

We employ Soft attention [14] to generate D-dimensional context vector $\hat{z}_t$. Context $\hat{z}_t$ of Current step is weighted sum of previous context by weight of α_t, which measures how much attention gain in each pixel:

$$\hat{z}_t = \alpha_t^T \cdot \mathbf{a} \tag{1}$$

α_t can be derived from hidden state h_t of previous time step.

$$e_{ti} = f_{att}(\mathbf{a}_i, h_{t-1}) \tag{2}$$

$$\alpha_{ti} = \frac{\exp(e_{ti})}{\sum \exp(e_{tk})} \tag{3}$$

e_{ti} stores information from previous time step where f_{att} is attention model.

4.2 Texture Analysis

Texture are also important in our analysis, to get a detailed description of the bedding area, we also extract texture feature to train our model. Gray Level Cooccurrence Matrix (GLCM) [19] is used to characterize the texture by quantifying differences between neighboring pixel values (vertically or horizontally) within a specified window of interest. Suppose the gray level has been quantized to N_g Levels [21]. GLCM defines a square matrix whose size is equal to the N_g. P_{ij} in the location (i, j) of the matrix means the co-occurrence probability for co-occurring pixels with gray levels i and j.

The GLCM features used were listed in table. Energy measures local uniformity. Contrast measures the local variations. Entropy reflects the degree of disorder in an image. Homogeneity Measures the closeness of the distribution of elements [21]. We extracted GLCM matrices using 4 different offsets (1, 2, 3 and 4 pixels) and phases (0°, 45°, 90°, 135°). SVM (support vector machines) [28] are used for classification of different texture classes (Table 1).

Table 1. The GLCM features used in this study.

Method	Formula
Energy	$\sum_{i,j=1}^{N_g} P_{ij}^2$
Contrast	$\sum_{i,j=1}^{N_g} P_{ij}(i-j)^2$
Entropy	$-\sum_{i,j=1}^{N_g} P_{ij} \log P_{ij}$
Homogeneity	$\sum_{i,j=1}^{N_g} \frac{P_{ij}}{1+(i-j)^2}$

4.3 Decoder

To generate the hidden state, we used LSTM [18] to simulate the memory of every time step based on context vector, previous hidden state and previous generated word. $i_t, f_t,$ c_t, o_t, h_t are the input, forget, memory, output and hidden state of the LSTM. Input i_t, output o_t and forget f_t controls other states, can be derived from the context vector z and hidden state of last hidden state.

$$\begin{pmatrix} i_t \\ f_t \\ o_t \\ g_t \end{pmatrix} = \begin{pmatrix} \sigma \\ \sigma \\ \sigma \\ \tanh \end{pmatrix} T_{D+m+n,n} \begin{pmatrix} Ey_{t-1} \\ h_{t-1} \\ \widehat{z}_t \end{pmatrix} \tag{4}$$

Input gate i_t, forget gate f_t, output gate o_t are activated by sigmoid function. Input modulation gate g_t is activated by tanh function. T denote an affine transformation with learned parameters. D, m and n are the dimension of feature vector, embedding and LSTM units respectively. E is an embedding matrix. y is the caption generated.

Memory c_t is the core of the LSTM, derived from memory of last word generated and g_t, the forget state f_t controls memory of previous word. $\odot$ is element-wise multiplication.

$$c_t = f_t \odot c_{t-1} + i_t \odot g_t \tag{5}$$

And hidden state h_t was calculated from memory and controlled by output o_t. Then use fully connected layer to generate current word y_t.

$$h_t = o_t \odot \tanh c_t \qquad (6)$$

5 Experiment

5.1 Data Collection

To train our model, we collect data from several sources: open dataset (Microsoft COCO), images collected from internet, and photos captured by us.

Microsoft COCO [23] is a large-scale object detection, segmentation, and captioning dataset. The Microsoft COCO 2014 captions dataset contains 82,783 training, 40,504 validation, and 40,775 testing images. It has variety of objects and scenes, from indoor to outdoor and annotated with sentence describe the scene. Each image has several corresponding annotations.

Although Microsoft COCO dataset works for majority of general Image captioning task, it still lake of some data that specialized for our scenario. To address this issue, we collected data that contains infant, cribs, soft objects, and bedding. Then manually annotate them. For example, in the scenario (a) "baby sleep on tummy" under Sect. 5.3 Experiment Result, note that each image doesn't have to include all the required information; just a subset of the needed information for each individual image is enough, in the event that the dataset overall covers every aspect. For example, we collected images where the baby is sleeping on his back, other images contained only crib with bedding, and some images contained different kind of bedding objects such as pillow, comforter and blanket.

In addition to Microsoft COCO dataset, we collected and annotated 1,843 images related to the baby's sleeping position. The corresponding annotation for those images indicated that 1,463 out of the 1,843 images included bedding objects. And 357 images contain comprehensive visual content which usually have multiple elements in single image.

5.2 Training

As aforementioned, we used pre-trained VGG net model to create annotation vector, and besides that, we also used SVM specialized in classify bedding from the texture feature extracted from image. Then we used the ratio in Microsoft COCO dataset to separate our own dataset into training, validation and test set. It took around 3 days to train the model on Nvidia Quodro K6000 GPU.

SVM is trained using subset of the dataset that contains only bedding materials. We've compared accuracy rate with applying texture classification with 5 layer CNN using raw input images. Experiment shows our GLCM feature based method achieved accuracy rate 95.48%, outperforms 5 layer CNN's result (68.72%) on our dataset.

5.3   Experiment Result

We blurred out infants' faces in input image out of privacy concern. It shows three typical scenarios. Attention map generated by attention model highlighted important regions where the algorithm focused on (Fig. 2).

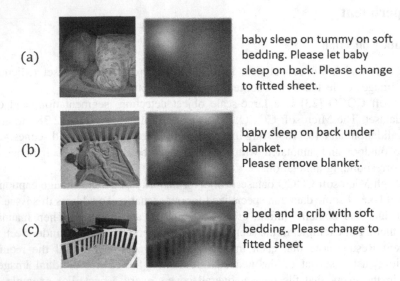

Fig. 2. Input image (first column), attention map (second column), caption generated

Captions generated from the image indicated the required information regarding to infant sleep position, soft object and bedding condition, and as post processing, it gives the instruction or advice to fix the detected issue. In Fig. 2(a), the generated caption "baby sleep on tummy on soft bedding" suggests the following two issues: 1. Wrong sleeping position; and 2. Inappropriate bedding material. After the machine translation step, the post processing generates specific instructions related to the detected issues, such as advising to "please let baby sleep on back"; or "please change to fitted sheet", etc. Similarly, the blanket in Fig. 2(b) was detected, which is also one of the common risk factors. In Fig. 2(c) when there is no infant in the picture, our method still can generate caption stated the issue of soft bedding by texture analysis. It is helpful to provide a safe infant sleeping environment.

To evaluate the result and to analyze how well it describes the issue in the given image, we calculated the precision rate and recall rate [27] of the result. When interpreting the result, a true positive means it successfully addressed the corresponding issue; and a false positive means it detected the issue that does not occur in the image; while a true negative means that there is no issue in the image, and the caption shows the same way; and finally, a false negative means that it missed an issue that occurred in the image (Table 2).

Table 2. Evaluation result

	Positive	Negative
True	61	5
False	14	8

The precision rate = True positive/(True positive + False positive) = 81.3%
The recall rate = True positive/(True positive + False negative) = 88.4%

6 Conclusion

We proposed a new framework of image captioning to help diagnosis the infant sleeping environment which is essential to reduce risk of SIDS. In addition to a general description, a detailed relevant information was generated in order to give a constructive advice accordingly. Most of the test set generated correct caption which addresses the potential danger factor that occurs in the image. The proposed method would achieve better performance with higher-quality extensive data. Although this method was applied on infant sleeping environment, it would also find real-world applications, such as in the case of real-world assistive systems and any other case where natural language is generated as the output and facilitates the interaction, making the human–computer interaction more convenient.

Acknowledgements. We greatly appreciate the collaboration with Dr. Rosemary Nabaweesi from University of Arkansas for Medical Sciences for helping us collect data and providing theoretical guidance on SIDS.

References

1. https://www1.nichd.nih.gov/sts/about/SIDS/Pages/default.aspx. Accessed 01 June 2018
2. https://www.cdc.gov/sids/data.htm. Accessed 01 June 2018
3. Kiros, R, Salakhutdinov, R., Zemel, R.S.: Unifying visual-semantic embeddings with multimodal neural language models. arXiv preprint arXiv:1411.2539 (2014)
4. Mao, J., Xu, W., Yang, Y., et al.: Deep captioning with multimodal recurrent neural networks (m-RNN). arXiv preprint arXiv:1412.6632 (2014)
5. Wu, Q., Shen, C., Liu, L., et al.: What value do explicit high level concepts have in vision to language problems? In: Proceedings of the IEEE Conference on Computer Vision and Pattern Recognition, pp. 203–212 (2016)
6. Liu, X., Milanova, M.: Visual attention in deep learning: a review. Int. Rob. Auto. J. 4(3), 154–155 (2018)
7. http://pediatrics.aappublications.org/content/early/2016/10/20/peds.2016-2938
8. https://store.nanit.com/. Accessed 01 June 2018
9. https://owletcare.com/. Accessed 01 June 2018
10. Fang, H., Gupta, S., Iandola, F., et al.: From captions to visual concepts and back. In: Proceedings of the IEEE Conference on Computer Vision And Pattern Recognition, pp. 1473–1482 (2015)

11. Karpathy, A., Fei-Fei, L.: Deep visual-semantic alignments for generating image descriptions. In: Proceedings of the IEEE Conference on Computer Vision and Pattern Recognition (2015)
12. Socher, R., Karpathy, A., Le, Q.V., et al.: Grounded compositional semantics for finding and describing images with sentences. Trans. Assoc. Comput. Linguist. 2(1), 207–218 (2014)
13. Vinyals, O., Toshev, A., Bengio, S., et al.: Show and tell: a neural image caption generator. In: 2015 IEEE Conference on Computer Vision and Pattern Recognition (CVPR), pp. 3156–3164. IEEE (2015)
14. Xu, K., Ba, J., Kiros, R., et al.: Show, attend and tell: Neural image caption generation with visual attention. In: International Conference on Machine Learning, pp. 2048–2057 (2015)
15. Cheng, M.M., Mitra, N.J., Huang, X., et al.: Global contrast based salient region detection. IEEE Trans. Patt. Anal. Mach. Intell. 37(3), 569–582 (2015)
16. Mnih, V., Heess, N., Graves, A.: Recurrent models of visual attention. In: Advances in Neural Information Processing Systems, pp. 2204–2212 (2014)
17. Ba, J., Mnih, V., Kavukcuoglu, K.: Multiple object recognition with visual attention. arXiv preprint arXiv:1412.7755 (2014)
18. Gers, F.A., Schmidhuber, J., Cummins, F.: Learning to forget: continual prediction with LSTM. Neural Comput. 12, 2451–2471 (2000)
19. Haralick, R.M., Shanmugam, K.: Textural features for image classification. IEEE Trans. Syst. Man Cybern. 6, 610–621 (1973)
20. Huang, X., Liu, X., Zhang, L.: A multichannel gray level co-occurrence matrix for multi/hyperspectral image texture representation. Remote Sens. 6(9), 8424–8445 (2014)
21. Soh, L.K., Tsatsoulis, C.: Texture analysis of SAR sea ice imagery using gray level co-occurrence matrices. IEEE Trans. Geosci. Remote Sens. 37(2), 780–795 (1999)
22. Simonyan, K., Zisserman, A.: Very deep convolutional networks for large-scale image recognition. arXiv preprint arXiv:1409.1556 (2014)
23. Chen, X., Fang, H., Lin, T.Y., et al.: Microsoft COCO captions: data collection and evaluation server. arXiv preprint arXiv:1504.00325 (2015)
24. Kulkarni, G., Premraj, V., Ordonez, V., et al.: Babytalk: understanding and generating simple image descriptions. IEEE Trans. Patt. Anal. Mach. Intell. 35(12), 2891–2903 (2013)
25. Mitchell, M., Han, X., Dodge, J., et al.: Midge: generating image descriptions from computer vision detections. In: Proceedings of the 13th Conference of the European Chapter of the Association for Computational Linguistics, pp. 747–756. Association for Computational Linguistics (2012)
26. Yang, Y., Teo, C.L., Daumé III, H., et al.: Corpus-guided sentence generation of natural images. In: Proceedings of the Conference on Empirical Methods in Natural Language Processing, pp. 444–454. Association for Computational Linguistics (2011)
27. Davis, J., Goadrich, M.: The relationship between Precision-Recall and ROC curves. In: Proceedings of the 23rd International Conference on Machine Learning, pp. 233–240. ACM (2006)
28. Hearst, M.A., Dumais, S.T., Osuna, E., et al.: Support vector machines. IEEE Intell. Syst. Appl. 13(4), 18–28 (1998)

A First-Person Vision Dataset of Office Activities

Girmaw Abebe[1]([⊠]), Andreu Catala[2], and Andrea Cavallaro[3]

[1] Institute of Biomedical Engineering, University of Oxford, Oxford, UK
girmaw.abebe@eng.ox.ac.uk
[2] Universitat Politecnica de Catalunya, Barcelona, Spain
andreu.catala@upc.edu
[3] Centre for Intelligent Sensing, Queen Mary University of London, London, UK
a.cavallaro@qmul.ac.uk

Abstract. We present a multi-subject first-person vision dataset of office activities. The dataset contains the highest number of subjects and activities compared to existing office activity datasets. Office activities include person-to-person interactions, such as chatting and handshaking, person-to-object interactions, such as using a computer or a whiteboard, as well as generic activities such as walking. The videos in the dataset present a number of challenges that, in addition to intra-class differences and inter-class similarities, include frames with illumination changes, motion blur, and lack of texture. Moreover, we present and discuss state-of-the-art features extracted from the dataset and baseline activity recognition results with a number of existing methods. The dataset is provided along with its annotation and the extracted features.

Keywords: Wearable camera · First-person vision · Dataset

1 Introduction

First-person vision (FPV) uses wearable cameras to record a scene from the point of view of the wearer. FPV applications include lifelogging, video summarisation, and activity recognition. Datasets are important to support the development and testing of algorithms and classification pipelines for FPV applications. Publicly available FPV datasets are mainly focused on activities such as cooking [4,6,15], sports [2,7], and ego-activities such as *going upstairs/downstairs* and *walking* [11]. Office-related activity datasets are instead limited in both number and range of activities [3,9,10,14].

The 2-hour office dataset (UTokyo) by Ogaki et al. [10] contains only five activities (*reading a book, watching a video, copying text from screen to screen, writing sentences on paper* and *browsing internet*) performed by five subjects and recorded with a head-mounted camera. Other activities (e.g. *conversing, singing* and *random head motions*) are considered part of a *void* class. Each subject recorded each activity for about two minutes twice, thus resulting 60 videos.

© Springer Nature Switzerland AG 2019
F. Schwenker and S. Scherer (Eds.): MPRSS 2018, LNAI 11377, pp. 27–37, 2019.
https://doi.org/10.1007/978-3-030-20984-1_3

An eye-tracker was used in addition to a GoPro Hero camera to help estimate the attention (gaze) of the wearer. The 30-minute NUS first-person dataset by Narayan et al. [9] covers eight interaction activities (*handshake, waving, throwing an object, passing an object, open and go through a door, using a cellphone, typing on a keyboard*, and *writing on a board/paper*) captured with a head-mounted GoPro camera and from a third-person perspective. The 13-minute life-logging egocentric activities (LENA) dataset by Song et al. [14] contains 13 activities performed by 10 subjects using Google Glass. Each subject recorded two 30-second clips for each activity. The activities are grouped as motion (*walking and running*), social interaction (e.g. *talking on a phone and to people*), office work (*writing, reading, watching videos, browsing internet*), food (*eating and drinking*) and house work. LENA includes different varieties of *walk* activity, which are *walk straight, walk back and forth* and *walk up/down*, as different activities, and challenges such as scene and illumination variations.

In this paper, we present FPV-O, a dataset of office activities in first-person vision available at http://www.eecs.qmul.ac.uk/~andrea/fpvo.html. FPV-O contains 20 activities performed by 12 subjects with a chest-mounted camera (see Fig. 1). The activities include three person-to-person interaction activities (*chat, shake* and *wave*), sixteen person-to-object interaction activities (*clean* and *write on a whiteboard, use a microwave; use a drink vending machine, take a drink from the vending machine, open* and *drink; use a mobile phone, read* and *typeset on a computer, take a printed paper, staple* and *skim over* and *handwrite on a paper, wash hands* and *dry*), and one proprioceptive activity (*walk*). The more stable chest-mount solution is often preferred [2,8,20,21] to the head-mount solution, which is affected by head motion [7,11]. The larger number of activities and subjects in FPV-O compared to other datasets create classification challenges due to intra-activity differences and inter-activity similarities (see Fig. 2). The dataset is distributed with its annotation and features extracted with both hand-crafted methods and deep learning architectures, as well as classification results with baseline classifiers. FPV-O includes around three hours of videos and contains the highest number of both subjects (12) and activities (20) compared to other office activity datasets. The dataset will be made available with the camera ready paper.

The paper is organized as follows. Section 2 provides the details of the FPV-O dataset, the definition and duration of the activities as well as the contribution of each subject to the dataset. Section 3 describes state-of-the-art features extracted for the recognition of activities in FPV. Section 4 presents the baseline results of the feature groups (and their concatenation) in classifying office activities. Finally, Sect. 5 concludes the paper.

2   The FPV-O Dataset

We used a chest-mounted GoPro Hero3+ camera with 128×720 resolution and 30 fps frame rate. Twelve subjects (nine male and three female) participated in the data collection. Each subject recorded a continuous video sequence of approximately 15 min on average, resulting in a total of 3 h of videos. The FPV-O activities (see Table 1) extend the scope of existing office activity datasets [9,10,14] by including, for example, more object-interactive activities such as *using a printer, microwave, drink vending machine, stapler, computer*, which are commonly performed in a typical office environment. The number of classes (20) is larger compared to existing office activity datasets [9,10,14] (Table 2).

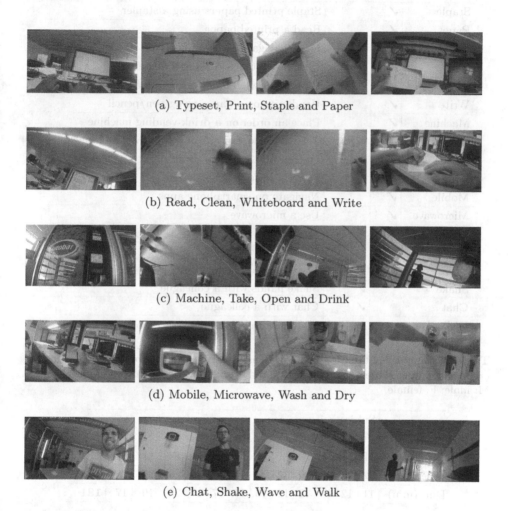

(a) Typeset, Print, Staple and Paper

(b) Read, Clean, Whiteboard and Write

(c) Machine, Take, Open and Drink

(d) Mobile, Microwave, Wash and Dry

(e) Chat, Shake, Wave and Walk

Fig. 1. Keyframes of activities from sample videos in the FPV-O dataset.

The detailed contribution of each subject in the FPV-O dataset for each class is given in Table 3. The annotation includes start and end times of each class segment for each video sequence. The ground-truth labels were generated using ELAN [16].

Table 1. Definition of activities in the FPV-O dataset. P-P: person-to-person interactions; P-O: person-to-object interactions; P: proprioceptive activity.

Label	Category P-O	P-P	P	Definition
Typeset	✓			Typeset using a computer keyboard
Print	✓			Take out a printed paper from a printer
Staple	✓			Staple printed papers using a stapler
Paper	✓			Read a printed paper
Read	✓			Read/navigate on a computer
Clean	✓			Clean a whiteboard using a duster
Whiteboard	✓			Write on a whiteboard using a marker
Write	✓			Handwrite on a paper using pen/pencil
Machine	✓			Place an order on a drink vending machine
Take	✓			Take a bottle/can out of a drink vending machine
Open	✓			Open a bottle/can to drink
Drink	✓			Drink, e.g. from a bottle/can
Mobile	✓			Navigate on smartphone apps
Microwave	✓			Use a microwave
Wash	✓			Wash hands
Dry	✓			Use a hand dryer
Wave		✓		Wave to a colleague
Shake		✓		Shake hands with a colleague
Chat		✓		Chat with a colleague
Walk			✓	Walk naturally

Table 2. Summary of the FPV-O dataset that describes the number of video segments (# segments) per subject, S_i, $i \in \{1, 12\}$, and overall duration (Dur.) in minutes (min). M: male; F: female.

	Subjects S_1	S_2	S_3	S_4	S_5	S_6	S_7	S_8	S_9	S_{10}	S_{11}	S_{12}	**Total**
Gender	M	M	M	F	M	M	M	F	M	F	M	M	**12**
# segments	32	27	28	29	32	29	27	36	25	26	27	26	**344**
Dur. (min)	11	12	11	12	12	16	17	17	17	20	19	17	**181**

The challenges in FPV-O include intra-activity differences, i.e. an activity performed differently by subjects due to their pose differences (see Fig. 2). Chest-mounting may also result in different field-of-views for male and female subjects (see Fig. 2a). Additional challenges include inter-activity similarities, e.g. *chat* and *shake* (Fig. 2b); *read* and *typeset* (Fig. 2c). Some of inter-activity similarities

Table 3. Details for the contribution of each subject, S_i, $i \in \{1, 12\}$, in FPV-O for each class in number of frames. Note that some activities are not performed by some subjects.

	Subjects												
	S_1	S_2	S_3	S_4	S_5	S_6	S_7	S_8	S_9	S_{10}	S_{11}	S_{12}	Total
Chat	550	1765	1722	1160	1420	2368	3419	1750	2045	3830	423	347	20799
Clean	499	243	236	671	597	1010	928	873	250	0	435	202	5944
Drink	338	216	145	101	207	288	145	555	88	179	52	35	2349
Dryer	646	1040	540	848	854	641	663	506	1060	1003	1453	0	9254
Machine	615	87	182	138	324	266	142	491	93	87	134	131	2690
Microwave	138	569	614	587	887	698	686	564	850	308	280	347	6528
Mobile	1818	2050	1061	0	2173	2697	2098	1972	3234	0	0	2781	19884
Open	104	0	0	0	0	0	0	0	42	0	0	0	146
Paper	470	1133	989	1510	2152	2415	2428	2590	3402	3405	1831	1921	24246
Print	149	108	153	98	110	155	108	110	121	119	109	0	1340
Read	938	1477	959	2446	1034	1792	2638	2590	1564	3159	4046	2242	24885
Shake	165	168	163	145	90	156	134	123	95	152	123	96	1610
Staple	33	249	63	249	271	454	105	99	194	129	0	0	1846
Take	191	138	93	99	111	147	169	108	109	163	147	85	1560
Typeset	1807	1319	1241	1079	1139	1888	3255	3090	3537	3114	3945	3147	28561
Walk	1116	1350	1292	2116	1872	2890	1707	1280	1200	2219	2023	2366	21431
Wash	474	464	213	234	683	567	427	363	700	333	525	0	4983
Wave	222	47	60	212	60	267	465	43	70	0	0	0	1446
Whiteboard	1043	2256	621	1905	1941	1828	2479	2525	3083	2821	2917	2448	25867
Write	1218	1648	1360	1412	0	1864	1785	2197	3294	2650	2634	2478	22540
Total	12534	16327	11707	15010	15925	22391	23781	21829	25031	23671	21077	18626	227909

could be avoided by merging them into a macro activity, e.g. *read* and *typeset* can be merged as *using a computer* activity. Some activities may occur only for a very short duration, e.g. *open* has only 146 frames, whereas *typeset* has 28, 561 frames (see Table 3). This exemplifies class imbalance in FPV-O as data-scarce activities, such as *open*, *wave* and *shake*, have limited information for training. There are also illumination changes as indoor lighting often mixes with daylight (Fig. 2d). Moreover, feature extraction is made challenging by motion blur and lack of texture (Fig. 2e).

3   The Features

We selected three frequently employed FPV-based existing methods to extract discriminant features for office activity classification in FPV-O. These are *average pooling* (AP) [17–19], *robust motion features* (RMF) [1,2] and *pooled appearance features* (PAF) [1,12], which we describe below.

Let $\mathbf{V} = (V_1, \cdots, V_n, \cdots, V_N)$ be N temporally ordered activity samples from a subject. Each sample, V_n, contains a window of L frames, i.e. $V_n = (f_{n,1}, f_{n,2}, \cdots f_{n,i}, \cdots f_{n,L})$. Successive V_n pairs may overlap. Each of AP, RMF and PAF provides a feature representation for V_n. AP and RMF mainly exploit motion using optical flow, whereas PAF encodes appearance information.

Grid optical flow of V_n is $G_n = (g_{n,1}, g_{n,2}, \cdots g_{n,i}, \cdots g_{n,L-1})$, where $g_{n,i} = g_{n,i}^x + jg_{n,i}^y$ represents a flow vector between successive frames, $f_{n,i}$ and $f_{n,i+1}$, $i \in [1, L - 1]$. The superscripts x and y represent horizontal and vertical components, respectively. γ is the number of grids in each of horizontal and vertical components, hence results γ^2 grids per frame. AP [18] applies average pooling

(a) Intra-activity differences among four *staple* clips

(b) Inter-activity similarity, e.g. *chat* (top row) and *shake* (bottom row)

(c) Inter-activity similarity, e.g. *read* (top row) and *typeset* (bottom row)

(d) Illumination changes

(e) Lack of texture and motion blur.

Fig. 2. Sample frames that illustrate the challenges in the FPV-O dataset.

of each element across $L - 1$ grid flow vectors in G_n, which helps discard noise. After smoothing, the final representation of AP is derived as a concatenation of the horizontal and vertical grid components.

RMF [2] extracts more discriminative features by encoding the direction, magnitude and frequency characteristics of G_n. RMF contains two parts: grid optical flow-based features (GOFF) and centroid-based virtual inertial features (VIF).

GOFF is extracted from the histogram and Fourier transform of motion direction, $G_n^\theta = arctan2(G_n^y/G_n^x)$, and motion magnitude, $|G_n| = \sqrt{|G_n^x|^2 + |G_n^y|^2}$. The histogram representations quantize G_n^θ and $|G_n|$ with β_d and β_m bins, respectively. The frequency representations are derived from grouping the frequency response magnitude of G_n^θ and $|G_n|$ into N_d and N_m bands, respectively. VIF is a virtual-inertial feature extracted from the movement of intensity centroid, $C_n = C_n^x + jC_n^y$, across frames in V_n. The intensity centroid is computed from first-order image moments as $C_n^x = \mathcal{M}_{O1}/\mathcal{M}_{OO}$ and $C_n^y = \mathcal{M}_{10}/\mathcal{M}_{OO}$. For a frame, $f_{n,i}$, which is H-pixels high and W-pixels wide, its first-order image moments are calculated from the weighted average of all the intensity values as $\mathcal{M}_{pq}^i = \sum_{r=1}^{H} \sum_{c=1}^{W} r^p c^q f_{n,i}(r,c)$, where $p, q \in \{0,1\}$. Once the centroid locations are computed across frames, C_n, then successive temporal derivatives are applied to obtain corresponding velocity, $\dot{C}_n$, and acceleration, $\ddot{C}_n$, components. VIF is extracted from $\dot{C}_n$ and $\ddot{C}_n$ as inertial features from accelerometer and gyroscope data, e.g. *minimum, maximum, energy, kurtosis, zero-crossing* and *low frequency coefficients*.

PAF [12] features are motivated by exploiting appearance features using different pooling operations. We test two types of appearance features: *Overfeat* and *HOG*. Overfeat [13] is a high-level appearance feature that is extracted from the last hidden layer of a deep convolutional neural network - Overfeat [13], which was pretrained with a large image dataset (ImageNet [5]). HOG (histogram of oriented gradients) is a commonly used frame-level appearance descriptor [1]. A simple averaging can be applied for each feature element in HOG and Overfeat across frames to obtain a representation for a video sample, V_n. Gradient pooling (GP) can also be applied to encode variation of the appearance features across frames. The gradient is computed by applying a first-order derivative on each feature element across time, and the pooling operations include sum and histogram of positive and negative gradients [12].

We follow the parameter setups for the corresponding methods as in their authors' choices. Hence, we used $L = 90$ frames (equivalent to three seconds duration) and $\gamma = 20$ for each of horizontal and vertical grid components. Thus AP becomes 800-D. For GOFF of RMF, $\beta_d = 36$, $\beta_m = 15$, $N_d = N_m = 25$, resulting 137-D feature vector. For VIF, we extracted 106-D feature vector that is composed of 60-D frequency features, i.e. 10-D low frequency coefficients from 6 inertial time-series components (2 velocity, 2 acceleration and their magnitude (2)). RMF concatenates GOFF and VIF resulting in 243-D feature vector. For PAF, HOG is 200-D extracted using 5-by-5-by-8 spatial and orientation bins. Overfeat [13] is extracted from the last hidden layer resulting 4096-D feature.

4   Baseline Classification Results

In this section, we describe the setups employed to validate different state-of-the-art features on the FPV-O dataset using multiple classifiers. The baseline results, evaluated using various performance metrics, are thoroughly discussed.

We employed support vectors machines (SVM) and k-nearest neighbours (KNN), which are the most frequently employed, respectively, parametric and non-parametric classifiers for activity recognition in FPV [2]. We apply one-vs-all (OVA) strategy for the training of SVM. Since FPV-O consists of 12 subjects, we experiment *one-subject-out* validation, which reserves one subject for testing and uses the remaining for training in each iteration.

We employ precision ($\mathcal{P}$), recall ($\mathcal{R}$) and F-score ($\mathcal{F}$) metrics to evaluate the classification performance. Other performance metrics such as accuracy and specificity are not used as they are less informative of the recognition performance in the OVA strategy [2]. Given true positives (TP), false positive (FP) and false negative (FN), the metrics are computed as $\mathcal{P} = \frac{TP}{TP+FP}$, $\mathcal{R} = \frac{TP}{TP+FN}$ and $\mathcal{F} = \frac{2*\mathcal{P}*\mathcal{R}}{\mathcal{P}+\mathcal{R}}$. For each one-subject-out iteration, $\mathcal{P}$, $\mathcal{R}$ and $\mathcal{F}$ are evaluated for each activity. The final recognition performance is computed by averaging, first, over all activities, and then over all subjects. The confusion matrix is also given to visualize the misclassification among activities. All experiments were conducted using Matlab2014b, i7-3770 CPU @ 3.40 GHz, Ubuntu 14.04 OS and 16 GB RAM.

Table 4. Performance of different state-of-the-art features on the FPV-O dataset with an SVM and a KNN classifier. The performance metrics are $\mathcal{P}$: precision; $\mathcal{R}$: recall and $\mathcal{F}$: F-score. Key – AP: average pooling; VIF: virtual inertial features; GOFF: grid optical flow-based features; RMF: robust motion features; PAF: pooled appearance features; GP: gradient pooling applied on the appearance features. RMF [2] + PAF [12] represents a concatenation of existing motion- and appearance-based features.

Features	SVM			KNN		
	$\mathcal{P}$	$\mathcal{R}$	$\mathcal{F}$	$\mathcal{P}$	$\mathcal{R}$	$\mathcal{F}$
AP [18]	17	10	10	15	10	9
VIF [2]	24	16	15	21	20	19
GOFF [2]	53	42	44	43	44	41
RMF [2]	51	38	41	45	43	41
PAF [12]	57	53	52	54	55	50
PAF-GP [12]	**61**	51	53	51	53	50
RMF [2] + PAF [12]	**61**	**56**	**56**	**55**	**57**	**52**

The performance of the selected methods on the FPV-O dataset is shown in Table 4. AP [17,18] only concatenates smoothed horizontal and vertical grid components, and does not use magnitude and direction information, which is important in this context. As a result, the performance of AP are the lowest both with SVM and KNN. RMF outperforms AP as it encodes motion magnitude, direction and dynamics, using multiple feature groups (GOFF and VIF). The performance of VIF of RMF are inferior to GOFF as the intensity centroid of a frame hardly changes over time since the subjects remain stationary for different activities, e.g. *read*, *mobile* and *typeset*. While both AP and RMF are designed to encode motion information in FPV-O, PAF exploits appearance information that is more discriminative for interaction-based activities. As a result, PAF has the highest performance among the selected methods. PAF achieves equivalent performance with and without gradient pooling (GP) (see Table 4). This also confirms the superiority of appearance information for this dataset as variation encoding using GP did not provide significantly discriminative characteristics. The concatenation of both motion and appearance features outperform all the remaining feature groups.

The confusion matrices shown in Fig. 3 replicate the corresponding performance of motion-based (RMF [2]), appearance-based (PAF-GP [12]) and

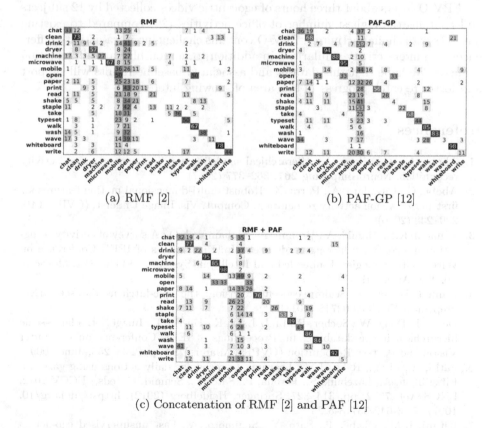

(a) RMF [2]   (b) PAF-GP [12]

(c) Concatenation of RMF [2] and PAF [12]

Fig. 3. Confusion matrices based on the SVM classifier using RMF [2], PAF-GP [12] and the concatenation of RMF and PAF.

their concatenation (RMF [2] + PAF [12]). The concatenation of RMF [2] and PAF [12] improved the recognition performance of *drink* from 9% with RMF and 7% with PAF-GP to 22%. The same is true for *print* whose recognition performance was improved from 11% with RMF and 56% with PAF-GP to 76% with the concatenation. On the other hand, the combination of motion and appearance features worsened the recognition performance of *write*. Note also the frequent misclassification with *open* due to the class imbalance problem (see Table 3).

5   Conclusions

We collected, annotated and distributed a dataset of 20 office activities from a first-person vision perspective (FPV-O) at http://www.eecs.qmul.ac.uk/~andrea/fpvo.html. Moreover, we employed and discussed state-of-the-art features extracted using both handcrafted methods and deep neural architectures, and baseline results of different feature groups using SVM and KNN classifiers.

FPV-O covers about three hours of egocentric videos collected by 12 subjects and contains the highest number of office activities (20) compared to existing datasets with similar activities. FPV-O contains challenging intra-activity differences and inter-activity similarities in addition to motion blur and illumination changes. We hope that this dataset and associated baseline results will support and foster research progress in this area of growing interest.

References

1. Abebe, G., Cavallaro, A.: Hierarchical modeling for first-person vision activity recognition. Neurocomputing **267**, 362–377 (2017)
2. Abebe, G., Cavallaro, A., Parra, X.: Robust multi-dimensional motion features for first-person vision activity recognition. Comput. Vis. Image Underst. (CVIU) **149**, 229–248 (2016)
3. Asnaoui, K.E., Hamid, A., Brahim, A., Mohammed, O.: A survey of activity recognition in egocentric lifelogging datasets. In: Proceedings of IEEE Conference on Wireless Technologies, Embedded and Intelligent Systems (WITS), Fez, Morocco, pp. 1–8, April 2017
4. Damen, D., et al.: Scaling egocentric vision: the epic-kitchens dataset. arXiv preprint arXiv:1804.02748 (2018)
5. Deng, J., Dong, W., Socher, R., Li, L.J., Li, K., Fei-Fei, L.: ImageNet: a large-scale hierarchical image database. In: Proceedings of IEEE Conference on Computer Vision and Pattern Recognition (CVPR), Miami, USA, pp. 248–255, June 2009
6. Fathi, A., Li, Y., Rehg, J.M.: Learning to recognize daily actions using gaze. In: Fitzgibbon, A., Lazebnik, S., Perona, P., Sato, Y., Schmid, C. (eds.) ECCV 2012. LNCS, vol. 7572, pp. 314–327. Springer, Heidelberg (2012). https://doi.org/10.1007/978-3-642-33718-5_23
7. Kitani, K.M., Okabe, T., Sato, Y., Sugimoto, A.: Fast unsupervised ego-action learning for first-person sports videos. In: Proceedings of IEEE Computer Vision and Pattern Recognition (CVPR), Colorado, USA, pp. 3241–3248, June 2011

8. Nam, Y., Rho, S., Lee, C.: Physical activity recognition using multiple sensors embedded in a wearable device. ACM Trans. Embed. Comput. Syst. **12**(2), 26:1–26:14 (2013)

9. Narayan, S., Kankanhalli, M.S., Ramakrishnan, K.R.: Action and interaction recognition in first-person videos. In: Proceedings of IEEE Computer Vision and Pattern Recognition Workshops (CVPRW), Columbus, USA, pp. 526–532, June 2014

10. Ogaki, K., Kitani, K.M., Sugano, Y., Sato, Y.: Coupling eye-motion and ego-motion features for first-person activity recognition. In: Proceedings of IEEE Computer Vision and Pattern Recognition Workshops (CVPRW), Providence, USA, pp. 1–7, June 2012

11. Poleg, Y., Ephrat, A., Peleg, S., Arora, C.: Compact CNN for indexing egocentric videos. In: Proceedings of IEEE Winter Conference on Applications of Computer Vision (WACV), New York, USA, pp. 1–9, March 2016

12. Ryoo, M.S., Rothrock, B., Matthies, L.: Pooled motion features for first-person videos. In: Proceedings of IEEE Computer Vision and Pattern Recognition (CVPR), Boston, USA, pp. 896–904, March 2015

13. Sermanet, P., Eigen, D., Zhang, X., Mathieu, M., Fergus, R., LeCun, Y.: Overfeat: integrated recognition, localization and detection using convolutional networks. In: Proceedings of International Conference on Learning Representations (ICLR), Banff, Canada, April 2014

14. Song, S., Chandrasekhar, V., Cheung, N.-M., Narayan, S., Li, L., Lim, J.-H.: Activity recognition in egocentric life-logging videos. In: Jawahar, C.V., Shan, S. (eds.) ACCV 2014. LNCS, vol. 9010, pp. 445–458. Springer, Cham (2015). https://doi.org/10.1007/978-3-319-16634-6_33

15. Spriggs, E.H., De La Torre, F., Hebert, M.: Temporal segmentation and activity classification from first-person sensing. In: Proceedings of IEEE Computer Vision and Pattern Recognition Workshops (CVPRW), Miami, USA, pp. 17–24, June 2009

16. Wittenburg, P., Brugman, H., Russel, A., Klassmann, A., Sloetjes, H.: ELAN: a professional framework for multimodality research. In: Proceedings of International Conference on Language Resources and Evaluation (LREC), Genoa, Italy, pp. 1556–1559, May 2006

17. Zhan, K., Faux, S., Ramos, F.: Multi-scale conditional random fields for first-person activity recognition. In: Proceedings of IEEE International Conference on Pervasive Computing and Communications (PerCom), Budapest, Hungary, pp. 51–59, March 2014

18. Zhan, K., Faux, S., Ramos, F.: Multi-scale conditional random fields for first-person activity recognition on elders and disabled patients. Pervasive Mobile Comput. **16**(Part B), 251–267 (2015)

19. Zhan, K., Ramos, F., Faux, S.: Activity recognition from a wearable camera. In: Proceedings of IEEE International Conference on Control Automation Robotics & Vision (ICARCV), Guangzhou, China, pp. 365–370, December 2012

20. Zhang, H., et al.: Physical activity recognition based on motion in images acquired by a wearable camera. Neurocomputing **74**(12), 2184–2192 (2011)

21. Zhang, H., Li, L., Jia, W., Fernstrom, J.D., Sclabassi, R.J., Sun, M.: Recognizing physical activity from ego-motion of a camera. In: Proceedings of IEEE International Conference on Engineering in Medicine and Biology Society (EMBC), Buenos Aires, Argentina, pp. 5569–5572, August 2010

Perceptual Judgments to Detect Computer Generated Forged Faces in Social Media

Suzan Anwar[1,2(✉)], Mariofanna Milanova[1], Mardin Anwer[2,3], and Anderson Banihirwe[1]

[1] University of Arkansas at Little Rock, Little Rock, USA
sxanwar@ualr.edu
[2] Salahaddin University, Erbil, Iraq
[3] Lebanese-French University, Erbil, Iraq

Abstract. There has been an increasing interest in developing methods for image representation learning, focused in particular on training deep neural networks to synthesize images. Generative adversarial networks (GANs) are used to apply face aging, to generate new viewpoints, or to alter face attributes like skin color. For forensics specifically on faces, some methods have been proposed to distinguish computer generated faces from natural ones and to detect face retouching. We propose to investigate techniques based on perceptual judgments to detect image/video manipulation produced by deep learning architectures. The main objectives of this study are: (1) To develop technique to make a distinction between Computer Generated and photographic faces based on Facial Expressions Analysis; (2) To develop entropy-based technique for forgery detection in Computer Generated (CG) human faces. The results show differences between emotions in both original and altered videos. These computed results were large and statistically significant. The results show that the entropy value for the altered videos is reduced comparing with the value of the original videos. Histograms of original frames have heavy tailed distribution, while in case of altered frames; the histograms are sharper due to the tiny values of images vertical and horizontal edges.

Keywords: Video manipulation · ASM · Face expression · Entropy based histogram

1 Introduction

With advances in computer vision and graphics, it has become possible to generate image/videos with realistic synthetic faces. Companies like Google, Baidu, Nvidia, Adobe and startups such as Voicecey have recently funded efforts to fabricate audio or video. These companies have released do-it yourself software and open source tools available on GitHub such as DeepFake. Currently in-use methods can generate manipulated videos in real time Face2Face, can synthesize video based on audio input or can artificially animate static images. New technologies allow users to edit facial expressions. This gained incredible attention in the context of fake-news discussions.

© Springer Nature Switzerland AG 2019
F. Schwenker and S. Scherer (Eds.): MPRSS 2018, LNAI 11377, pp. 38–48, 2019.
https://doi.org/10.1007/978-3-030-20984-1_4

The results are raising concerns that face swaps technology can be used to spread misleading information.

According recent publication [1] "Right now, there is no tool that works all the time" says Mikel Rodriguez, a researcher in Mitre DCorp. The overview of face image synthesis approaches using deep learning techniques is presented in [2]. Most of the techniques used to swap faces generate an output as a face image or 3D facemask. For instance, it was virtually impossible to distinguish between the real Paul Walker and the computer-generated one in the film "The Fast and the Furious 7". The death of the actor during filming led the director to use previously recorded digital 3D scan data to reconstruct Mr. Walker's face for the unfinished scenes. Another example is Pro Evolution Soccer2, a video game developed and published by Konami. Since the 2012 version, the images of the soccer players are rendered so realistically that they look almost like real people [3].

In June, 2017 NVIDIA created a GAN that used CelebA-HQ's database of photos of famous people to generate images of people who don't actually exist. In 2018 NVIDIA proposed a new GAN that increases the variation in generated images [4]. GANs are used to apply face aging, to generate new viewpoints, or to alter face attributes like skin color [5].

Virtual Worlds have been used constructively for the benefit of the society. However, there are safety and security concerns as well e.g. cyberterrorism activities, child pornography detection and economic crimes such as money laundering.

Unreal images and videos can be used to harm people or to gain political and/or economic advantage. For example, fake images or videos about aliens, disasters, statesmen, or businessmen can create confusion or change people's' opinions. Social media platforms such as Facebook, Twitter, Flickr, or YouTube are ideal environments to widely disseminate these fake images and videos.

To combat this threat, CG manipulation-detection software will need to become more sophisticated and useful in the future. This technology, along with robust training and clear guidelines about what is acceptable, will enable media organizations to hold the line against willful image manipulation, thus maintaining their credibility and reputation as purveyors of the truth. The challenges to create new technologies are:

1. The algorithms used to fabricate images/video are based on convolutional neural network, widely used in object recognition. In Deep learning approach, features are automatically learned from training samples rather than being manually designed. However deep learning – based approaches are using mostly supervised learning. Although deep-learning-based approaches are promising, they are not yet mature in digital image forensics; a considerable amount of work remains to be done in this area.
2. Lack of sharing datasets, maintenance, and availability. Coming to a world where everything is connected (IoT) there is a need to collect data from streaming devices, such as Roku or AppleTV and Unmanned Aerial Vehicle (UAV) and variations of computer-generated images using new deep learning architectures.

We propose to investigate techniques based on perceptual judgments to detect image/video manipulation produced by deep learning architectures. The main objectives of this study are:

- To develop techniques to make a distinction between computer generated and photographic faces based on facial expressions analysis. The hypothesis is that facial emotions expressed by humans and facial expressions generated from fake faces are different. Humans can produce a large variety of facial expressions with a high range of intensities.
- To develop entropy based technique for forgery detection in CG human faces. The hypotheses is that natural images have some special properties different from the other types of images.

2   Related Work

Given the need for automated real-time verification of the digital image/video content, several techniques have been presented by researchers. There are two major categories of digital image treatment detection approaches: active approaches and passive approaches. Active approaches involve various kinds of watermarks or fingerprints of the image content and embedding them into the digital image [6]. With rising number of images used in social networks, it is impossible to require all the digital images on the internet to be watermarked before distribution. Therefore, passive forensics approaches have become a more popular choice.

Passive approaches detect changes in digital image by analyzing specific inherent clues or patterns that occur during the modification stage of digital images. Passive approaches do not rely on any prior or preset information and they have a broader application in image forensics. These techniques are successfully applied for tracking true and false news. In [7] the traces are classified in three groups: traces left in image acquisition, traces left in image storage, and traces left in image editing. Recently new category becomes popular images generated by computer graphics software.

For forensics specifically on faces, some methods have been proposed to distinguish computer generated faces from natural ones [8] and to detect face retouching [9]. In biometry, two pre-trained deep CNNs, VGG19 and AlexNet are proposed to detect morphed faces [10]. In [11] the authors proposed detection of two different face swapping manipulations using a two-stream network: one stream detects low-level inconsistencies between image patches while the other stream explicitly detects tampered faces.

Researchers from the Technical University of Munich have developed a deep learning algorithm that potentially identifies forged videos of face swaps on the internet. They trained the algorithm using a large set of face swaps that they made themselves, creating the largest database of these kinds of images available. They then trained the algorithm, called XceptionNet, to detect the face swaps [12].

In [13] different algorithms to detect and classify original and manipulated video are presented. In fact, this is difficult task for humans and computers alike, especially when the videos are compressed and have low resolution, as it often happens on social media. The authors also present a large-scale video dataset called "Face Forensics".

Some forgery detection methods also use statistical features to detect forgery. This technology is based on methods using natural image statistics. Natural images have some special properties different from the other types of images [14]. In [15] CG faces and real faces are discriminated by analyzing the variation of facial expressions in a video by analyzing sets of feature points.

3 Facial Emotion

In the experiments, the software FaceXpress which proposed in [16] is used to recognize the emotion for each frame within the FaceForansic dataset. The software starts with deting the face using Viola-Jones detector, followed by indicating 116 face landmarks using a multi resolution tracker Active Shape Model (ASM) tracker [17]. FaceXpress detects facial triangulation points using Active Shape Model tracker (see Fig. 1). Attributes are obtained by measuring the length of among the detected facial triangulation points. For some attributes such as, mouth width, mouth height, and the distance of the midpoint of eye gap to eyebrow midpoints, are obtained using Mahalanobis distance. The other attributes such as, the domain of vertical edge in the forehead and domain of horizontal edge in the mid forehead are obtained by filtering with Gauss core. The tracking point's location is used to compute the changes in facial regions such as eye brow wrinkles, forehead wrinkles, wrinkles in cheeks, distance eye to eyebrows, and vertical and horizontal measures of mouth [18] (see Fig. 2). Finally, a support vector machine (SVM) is used identified the detected facial emotion among the seven universal emotions; surprise, anger, happiness, sadness, fear, disgust, and neutral.

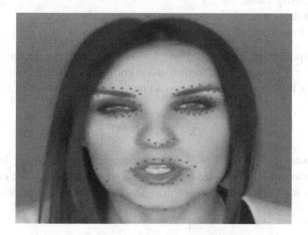

Fig. 1. Facial landmarks detection using ASM tracker

Fig. 2. Facial attributes that are used to detect the regions of interest

4 Entropy Based Histogram

Histogram processing includes image altering by modifying its histogram. To make the histogram of an image flat, normalization process is performed on both original and altered images from FaceForensics dataset (see Sect. 5.1). This process is called contrast enhancement where the function of intensity transformation based on information such as compression, description, and segmentation, are extracted. To compute the histogram of an image, the following discrete function is applied for intensity levels within [0, L−1] range.

$$h(r_k) = n_k \tag{1}$$

r_k is the intensity value,
n_k is the number of pixels in the image with intensity r_k,
$h(n_k)$ is the histogram of the digital image with Gray level r_k.

The total number of pixels is used for normalizing the image histogram by assuming an M × N image. This normalization computation is related to r_k probability of occurrence in the image. The equation to normalize the histogram is given below:

$$p(r_k) = \frac{n_k}{MN}, K = 0, 1, 2, \ldots\ldots L - 1 \tag{2}$$

$p(n_k)$ computes the probability of occurrence estimation of image level r_k.

The summation of all normalized histogram components should be equal to 1 [19]. The histograms for same frames in both original and altered videos are different (see Fig. 3).

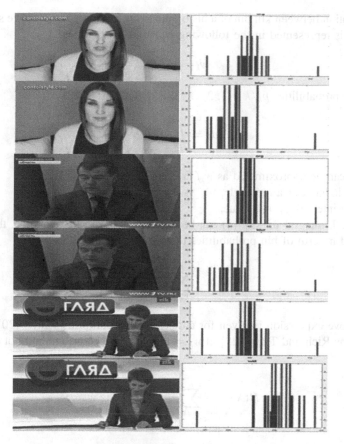

Fig. 3. Results of applying image histogram on both original and altered frames

Histograms of original frames have heavy tailed distribution. In case of altered frames, the histograms are sharper due to the tiny values of images vertical and horizontal edges. Also, an image mean information or entropy is determined from the images histogram. The purpose of computing the images entropy is to find its automatic focusing. For any random variable X, with probability density function f(x), the entropy definition is:

$$H(X) = -E[log\, f(X)] = -\int f(x) log\, f(x) dx \qquad (3)$$

The range of the variable is divided into n intervals (l_k, u_k), $k = 1, 2, \ldots, n$. The relation between the above entropy definition and the density that is represented as a histogram is shown in the following equation:

$$H(X) = -\sum_{k=1}^{n} \int_{l_k}^{u_k} f(x) log\, f(x) dx \qquad (4)$$

The relation between kth bin of a histogram to the kth term of the above summation with width is represented in the following equation:

$$w_k = u_k - l_k \tag{5}$$

The bin probabilities p_k, $k = 1, 2, \ldots n$ is defined as:

$$p_k = \int_{l_k}^{u_k} f(x)dx \tag{6}$$

Which can be approximated as $w_k f(x_k)$, where:
$f(x_k)$ is the area of a rectangle,
x_k is the interval (l_k, u_k) value,
To the kth integral for Eq. (4) can be approximated as $w_k f(x_k)log(x_k)$, this expression is used in term of bin probabilities to rewrite the entropy as:

$$H(X) = -\sum_{k=1}^{n} p_k log(p_k/w_k) \tag{7}$$

The above expression is given for a discrete distribution by Harris [20] and for a histogram by Rich and Tracy [21], if $w_k = 1$. When w_k is constant and not equal to 1, we used:

$$H(X) = -\sum_{k=1}^{n} p_k \, log \, p_k + log \, w \tag{8}$$

5 Results

5.1 FaceForensic Video Dataset

In this paper, we used the faceForansics video dataset [13] which consists of about 500.000 faces frames from around 1004 videos was collected from YouTube. The dataset has been manipulated using state-of-the-art face editing approach including classification and segmentation. The original face2face reenactment approach is used where the mouth interiors is selected from a mouth database depending on the target expression.

5.2 Facial Emotion

The FaceXpress software produces a csv file contains the recognized emotion for each frame for original and altered videos. To evaluate the differences in emotion between the original and altered videos, the mean square error (MSE) is the mean square error between the original and the altered video [22] from FaceForensic dataset. The metric

MSE between the produced emotions stored in the csv files for both original and altered videos is computed. For each frame in the original and altered video, the difference in emotion was squared and averaged. Table 1 shows the result of computing MSE for some videos' frames in the FaceForensic dataset, the results are dreadful and noticeable. By applying the FaceXpress software on some FaceForensic's videos, the results show a clear difference between emotions express in original and altered videos (see Fig. 4).

Fig. 4. Result of applying FaceXpress on some FaceForensic videos

Table 1. Results of MSE calculating

Video	MSE mean square error
v1	43.12965
v2	494.748
v3	420.4217
v4	224.6175
v5	327.7263
v6	96.96217
v7	322.4336
v8	172.4224
v9	367.1219
v10	366.6556
v11	306.3773
v12	123.6393
v13	22.05341
v14	162.6497
v15	38.28153
v101	168.4492
v102	226.1895
v148	113.8129
v149	29.48472
v150	364.4547

5.3 Entropy Based Histogram

Another measurement for image quality evaluation is computing the value of Entropy for both original and altered videos. We applied the entropy formula represented in Eq. 8, on both original and altered videos for the same frames. Table 2 shows that the entropy values for the altered frames are reduced comparing with their values for original videos.

Table 2. Results of computing Entropy value for three selected frames

Frame	Entropy value	
	Original	Altered
1	3.9122	3.8919
2	3.9114	3.8922
3	3.9106	3.8924

6 Conclusion

In this paper, we applied two different methods to test the quality and differences in emotions in FaceForensic original and altered videos dataset. In the first method, we used FaceXpress software to recognize the emotions in the videos for comparison. The differences in emotions between both original and altered videos are calculated using MSE measurement. The results of MSE values concluded that the differences in emotion are clear and noticeable between both original and altered videos. In the second method, we compute the Entropy values that are generated from the frame's histogram to test the quality of the videos. The result for the second method showed that the Entropy values for the altered videos are reduced comparing with their value for the original videos. Histograms of original frames have heavy tailed distribution, while in case of altered frames; the histograms are sharper due to the tiny values of images vertical and horizontal edges.

References

1. Nordrum, A.: Forging voices and faces. Spectrum IEEE 14–15, May 2018. https://doi.org/10.1109/mspec.2018.8352562
2. Lu, Z., Li, Z., Cao, J., He, R., Sun, Z.: Recent progress of face image synthesis (2017). https://arxiv.org/abs/1706.047173
3. Face-Swapping Porn: How a Creepy Internet Trend Could Threaten Democracy, Rolling Stone, 4.18.18. https://www.rollingstone.com/culture/features/face-swapping-porn-how-creepy-trend-could-threaten-democracy-w518929
4. Karras, T., Aila, T., Laine, S., Lehtinen, J.: Progressive Growing of GANs for Improved Quality, Stability, and Variation, ICLR 2018. http://research.nvidia.com/publication/2017-10_Progressive-Growing-of
5. Antipov, G., Baccouche, M., Dugelay, J.-L.: Face Aging With Conditional Generative Adversarial Networks, May 2017. https://arxiv.org/abs/1702.01983
6. Milanova, M., Kountchev, R., Ford, C., Kountcheva, R.: Watermarking with inverse difference pyramid decomposition. In: International Signal Processing Conference, Dallas, USA, pp. 346–362 (2003)
7. Lin, X., et al.: Recent advances in passive digital image security forensics: a brief review. Engineering 4, 29–39 (2018)
8. Rahmouni, N., Nozick, V., Yamagishi, J., Echizeny, I.: Distinguishing computer graphics from natural images using convolution neural networks. In: IEEE Workshop on Information Forensics and Security, pp. 1–6 (2017)
9. Bharati, A., Singh, R., Vatsa, M., Bowyer, K.: Detecting facial retouching using supervised deep learning. IEEE Trans. Inf. Forensics Secur. 11(9), 1903–1913 (2016)
10. Raghavendra, R., Raja, K., Venkatesh, S., Busch, C.: Transferable Deep-CNN features for detecting digital and print-scanned morphed face images. In: IEEE Computer Vision and Pattern Recognition Workshops, pp. 10–18 (2017)
11. Zhou, P., Han, X., Morariu, V., Davis, L.: Two-stream neural networks for tampered face detection. In: IEEE Computer Vision and Pattern Recognition Workshops, pp. 1831–1839 (2017)
12. https://www.engadget.com/2018/04/11/machine-learning-face-swaps-xceptionnet/

13. Rössler, A., Cozzolino, D., Verdoliva, L., Riess, C., Thies, J., Nießner, M.: FaceForensics: a large scale video dataset for forgery detection in human faces. CV Cornell University Library, March 2018
14. Souza, D., Yampolskiy, R.: Natural vs artificial face classification using uniform local directional patterns and wavelet uniform local directional patterns. In: IEEE CVPRW, pp. 27–33 (2014)
15. Dang-Nguyen, D.-T.: Discrimination of Computer Generated versus Natural Human Faces, February 2014. http://eprints-phd.biblio.unitn.it/1168/
16. Anwar, S., Milanova, M.: Real time face expression recognition of children with autism. IAEMR 1(1) (2016)
17. Cootes, T.F., Taylor, C.J., Cooper, D.H., Graham, J., et al.: Active shape models-their training and application. Comput. Vis. Image Underst. 61, 38–59 (1995)
18. Ekman, P., Friesen, W.: Facial Action Coding System. Consulting Psychologists Press, Palo Alto (1978)
19. Vij, K., Singh, Y.: Enhancement of images using histogram processing techniques. Int. J. Comput. Tech. Appl. 2(2), 309–313. ISSN: 2229-6093
20. Harris, B.: Entropy. In: Balakrishnan, N., Read, C.B., Vidakovic, B. (eds.) Encyclopedia of Statistical Sciences, vol. 3, 2nd edn., pp. 1992–1996. Wiley, New York (2006)
21. Rich, R., Tracy, J.: The relationship between expected inflation, disagreement, and uncertainty: evidence from matched point and density forecasts. Staff Report No. 253, Federal Reserve Bank of New York. (Revised version published in Review of Economics and Statistics 92(2010), 200–207 (2006)
22. http://homepages.inf.ed.ac.uk/rbf/CVonline/LOCAL_COPIES/VELDHUIZEN/node18.html

Combining Deep and Hand-Crafted Features for Audio-Based Pain Intensity Classification

Patrick Thiam[(✉)] and Friedhelm Schwenker

Institute of Neural Information Processing, Ulm University,
James-Franck-Ring, 89081 Ulm, Germany
{patrick.thiam,friedhelm.schwenker}@uni-ulm.de

Abstract. In this work, the classification of pain intensity based on recorded breathing sounds is addressed. A classification approach is proposed and assessed, based on hand-crafted features and spectrograms extracted from the audio recordings. The goal is to use a combination of feature learning (based on deep neural networks) and feature engineering (based on expert knowledge) in order to improve the performance of the classification system. The assessment is performed on the *SenseEmotion Database* and the experimental results point to the relevance of such a classification approach.

Keywords: Pain intensity classification · Deep neural networks · Random forests · Information fusion

1 Introduction

Most recently, the affective computing research community [9,10,14,28] has been very active in the domain of pain intensity classification [15,25]. Several datasets [2,20,30] relevant to this area of research have been made available lately and countless studies have investigated approaches to improve the robustness and the performance of automatic pain intensity classification systems [6,13,15,31]. However, these studies mostly focus on video and bio-physiological modalities. Therefore, the following work assesses the audio modality as a potentially cheap and relevant channel for pain intensity classification. The assessment consists of a combination of classical hand-crafted features (e.g. MFCCs) with learned representations extracted via deep neural networks. Approaches involving deep features have been already used in the domain of speech emotion recognition [4,18,19], and facial emotion recognition [17,23,32], with very promising results. Therefore, the current work aims at improving the performance as well as the robustness of a pain intensity classification system based on recorded breathing sounds by combining both hand-crafted and deep features.

The remainder of this work is organised as follows. In Sect. 2, a description of the proposed approach is provided. Section 3 consists of the description of the

© Springer Nature Switzerland AG 2019
F. Schwenker and S. Scherer (Eds.): MPRSS 2018, LNAI 11377, pp. 49–58, 2019.
https://doi.org/10.1007/978-3-030-20984-1_5

dataset, as well as the undertaken experiments and the corresponding results. Finally, the work is concluded in Sect. 4 with a short discussion about the presented results and planed future works.

2   Method Description

In the following section, a description of the proposed pain intensity classification approach based on audio recordings of breathing sounds is provided.

The proposed approach aims at using the complementarity of information encoded in both hand-crafted features and spectral representations of audio signals in order to improve the robustness as well as the performance of a pain intensity classification system. Therefore, feature learning consisting of a recurrent convolution neural network which uses spectrograms as visual representations of audio signals is performed. The resulting deep features are further combined with hand-crafted features in order to perform the classification of breathing sounds, in order to distinguish between breathing patterns in response to painful or pain free stimuli.

Spectrograms. A spectrogram is a 2-dimensional (time-frequency) visual representation of a signal, depicting the change in energy in a specific set of frequency bands over time. The abscissa of the visual representation usually corresponds to the temporal axis, while the ordinate corresponds to the frequency bands. The third dimension consisting of the energy in each frequency band over time is encoded in the brightness of the colors of the representation, with low energies represented by dark colors and high energies represented by brighter colors (see Fig. 1).

(a)   (b)

Fig. 1. (a) Raw audio signal. (b) Mel-scaled STFT Spectrogram. The darker the color, the lower the energy in the corresponding frequency band.

In the current work, Mel-scaled short-time Fourier transform spectrograms are used as visual representations of the audio signals. They are computed by first applying a short-time Fourier transform (STFT) to the raw audio signals, and subsequently mapping the resulting spectrogram onto the Mel scale. The spectrograms are extracted using the audio signals analysis tool librosa [21].

Convolutional Neural Networks. Convolutional neural networks (CNNs) correspond to a category of biologically inspired neural networks, consisting of a stack of different layers, which sequentially process some input data and exploit the feedback stemming from the expected output (ground-truth) in order to extract relevant information that can be used to solve a specific classification or regression task. The basic layers involved in CNNs are convolutional layers, pooling layers and fully-connected (FC) layers. Convolutional layers represent a set of filters which are automatically learned during the training process of CNNs. These layers extract relevant information in the form of feature maps, that are obtained by convolving the input data using the corresponding set of filters. These feature maps are subsequently used as input for the next layer in the architecture of the designed CNN. Pooling layers reduce the spatial resolution as well as the dimensionality of the feature maps while retaining the most relevant information in relation to the task at hand. The fully-connected layers are similar to multi-layer perceptrons (MLPs), and act as the classifier.

Given a large set of annotated samples, CNNs are known to be very effective in finding abstract representations of input data, that are suitable for the corresponding classification tasks and are able, in many cases, to significantly outperform well established hand-crafted (engineered) features.

Long Short-Term Memory Networks. Long short-term memory (LSTM) networks [12] correspond to a category of recurrent neural networks (RNNs) capable of learning long-term dependencies in sequential data, while addressing the vanishing (resp. exploding) gradient problem of standard RNNs [11]. This is achieved throughout the use of the so called memory cells, which are a key characteristic of LSTMs. The amount of information flowing through a LSTM network is regulated by the cell state throughout the use of three principal gates: forget gate, input gate and output gate. These gates are basically sigmoid layers with a point-wise multiplication operation. In this way, since the output of a layer is in the range $[0, 1]$, the gates control the amount of information that flows throughout the cell state. Keras [5] and TensorFlow [1] are used for the implementation of both CNNs and LSTMs in the current work.

Proposed Approach. An overview of the proposed approach is depicted in Fig. 2. The goal is to combine hand-crafted features based on expert knowledge and learned features based on deep neural networks in order to improve the performance of a classification system. Therefore, spectrograms are generated from the raw audio signals and segmented into non-overlapping windows. Furthermore, a spatio-temporal feature representation is learned from the segmented spectrograms, using a combination of time-distributed CNN and bidirectional LSTM. The spatial representation learned by the CNN is fed to the bidirectional LSTM, which in turn learns the temporal dependency between subsequent spectrogram windows in order to generate an adequate spatio-temporal representation of the input data.

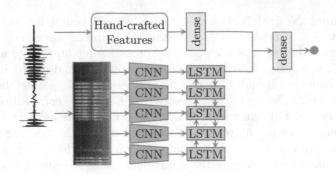

Fig. 2. Fusion architecture.

Meanwhile, hand-crafted features (e.g. MFCCs) are extracted from the audio signal and fed into a dense architecture consisting of several fully-connected layers. The resulting abstract representation is further concatenated with the learned features and fed to another dense architecture, which performs the classification. The whole architecture is subsequently trained end-to-end via backpropagation. Once the architecture has been trained, it can be use as a feature extraction network and the final dense layer can be replaced by a more conventional classifier (e.g. SVM). In the current work, we assess both approaches (once with a dense layer as classifier and once by replacing the dense layer of the pre-trained model by a conventional classifier) and replace the final dense layer with a random forest classifier [3]. The whole assessment is performed using Scikit-learn [22].

3   Experiments and Results

In the following section, a short description of the dataset, upon which the current work is built, is provided. Furthermore, the undertaken experiments are illustrated, followed by the description of the yielded results.

3.1   Dataset Description

The current work is based on the *SenseEmotion Database* (the reader is referred to [29], for more details about this specific dataset). It consists of 45 participants, each subjected to a series of artificially induced pain stimuli through temperature elevation (heat stimuli). Several modalities were synchronously recorded during the conducted experiments including audio streams, high resolution video streams, respiration, electromyography, electrocardiography, and electrodermal activity.

The experiments were conducted in two sessions with the heat stimuli induced during each session on one specific forearm (once left and once right). Each session lasted approximately 40 min and consisted of randomized temperature elevation between three individually pre-calibrated and gradually increasing temperatures (T_1: threshold temperature, T_2: intermediate temperature; T_3: tolerance temperature). A baseline temperature (T_0) was set for all participants to $32\,°C$ and corresponds to a pain free level of stimulation. Each of the four temperatures were randomly induced 30 times following the scheme depicted in Fig. 3.

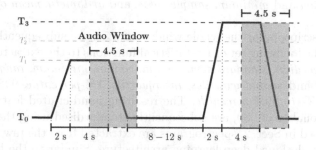

Fig. 3. Artificially induced pain stimuli through temperature elevation. T_0: baseline temperature ($32\,°C$); T_1: threshold temperature; T_2: intermediate temperature; T_3: tolerance temperature. The spectrogram and hand-crafted features are extracted from a window of length 4.5 s with a temporal shift of 4 s from the stimuli onsets.

Because of missing and erroneous data, 5 participants are excluded from the current assessment. Moreover, the current work focuses uniquely on the recorded audio streams (for some assessment including the other modalities, the reader is referred to [16,26,27]). Furthermore, the assessment performed consists of the classification task T_0 vs. T_3 (no pain vs. pain). Therefore, each dataset specific to the forearm on which the stimuli were elicited (left and right forearms) consists of approximately $2 \times 30 \times 40 = 2400$ recordings of breathing sounds, each recording consisting of a 4.5 s window extracted 4 s after the temperature elicitation onset (see Fig. 3) as proposed in [26], with its label corresponding to the level of heat stimulation. During the conducted experiments, three audio streams were synchronously recorded at a fixed sample rate of 48 kHz, using a digital wireless headset microphone, a directional microphone and the integrated microphone of the Microsoft Kinect v2. The recorded data consists uniquely of breathing and sporadic moaning sounds, since there were no verbal interaction involved in the experiments. The current work is based on the audio streams recorded by the wireless headset, since it was able to capture the emitted breathing an moaning sounds at a satisfactory extent.

3.2 Feature Extraction

The extracted hand-crafted features consist of a set of commonly used low level descriptors, extracted using the openSMILE feature extraction toolkit [8]. The features were extracted from 25 ms frames with a 10 ms shift between consecutive frames and comprise 13 *Mel Frequency Cepstral Coefficients* (MFCCs), each combined with its first and second order temporal derivatives, 6 *Relative Spectral Perceptual Linear Predictive* (RASTA-PLP) coefficients, each in combination with its first and second temporal derivatives, and 13 descriptors from the temporal domain (*root mean square signal energy, logarithmic signal energy*, each in combination with its first and second order temporal derivatives, *loudness contour, zero crossing rate, mean crossing rate, maximum absolute sample value, maximum* and *minimum sample value*, and *arithmetic mean of the sample values*).

Global descriptors for the whole window of 4.5 s are subsequently generated by applying the following set of 14 statistical functions to the extracted set of features: *mean, median, standard deviation, maximum, minimum, range, skewness, kurtosis, first* and *second quartiles, interquartile, 1%-percentile, 99%-percentile, range from 1%- to 99%-percentile*. The resulting hand-crafted features, with a total dimensionality of 980, are subsequently standardised using the z-score.

As described in Sect. 2, spectrograms are extracted from the raw audio signal and fed to the designed deep learning architecture. Similar to the hand-crafted features, spectrograms are generated from frames of length 25 ms with a shift of 10 ms between consecutive frames. Subsequently, the resulting STFT spectra are first converted to a logarithmic scale (decibels) and mapped into the Mel scale using 128 Mel bands. The resulting 2 dimensional representation is segmented into a total of 5 non-overlapping windows. The windows are scaled into RGB images with the fixed dimensionality 100×100 and normalised in the range $[0, 1]$. Therefore, the deep architecture has an input consisting of segments with the dimensionality $5 \times 100 \times 100 \times 3$ (since we are dealing with RGB images).

3.3 Network Settings

The designed architecture is assessed by comparing its performance with a dense architecture based uniquely on the hand-crafted features, a deep architecture based uniquely on the spectrograms and a late fusion of both architectures using a basic average score pooling. In each case, since the amount of data is very limited, the dropout [24] regularisation technique is applied to reduce over-fitting. Each architecture is trained using the Adam [7] optimisation algorithm, in combination with the binary cross-entropy loss function and a fixed batch size of 32.

The dense architecture for the classification based uniquely on the hand-crafted features comprises three fully-connected layers consisting of 300, 150 and 1 neurons respectively. The first two layers use rectified linear units (ReLU) as activation functions while the last layer uses a sigmoid activation function. Each of the first two layers is followed by a dropout layer with a dropout ratio of 50%. The whole architecture is trained for a total of 100 epochs with a fixed learning rate of 10^{-5}.

The deep architecture based on the spectrograms comprises a time-distributed CNN combined with a single layer bidirectional LSTM. The time-distributed CNN consists of two convolutional layers, with respectively 32 and 64 filters. An identical kernel size of 5×5, with the stride 2×2 is used in both layers, and similarly to the previous architecture, ReLU is used as activation function in both layers. Each convolutional layer is subsequently followed by a max pooling layer of size 2×2 and stride 2×2, and a dropout layer with a dropout ratio of 50%. The resulting spatial representation is fed to a bidirectional LSTM with 32 nodes. The resulting spatio-temporal representation is subsequently fed to a dense architecture consisting of a single fully-connected layer with 1 neuron and a sigmoid activation function. The whole architecture is trained for 150 epoches with a fixed learning rate of 10^{-4}.

Finally, the proposed architecture is designed by combining the spatio-temporal representation generated by the LSTM layer in the previous model with the features generated by the second fully-connected layer of the hand-crafted classification architecture, which results in a feature vector with the dimensionality $64 + 150 = 214$. The resulting representation is fed to a single fully-connected layer consisting of 1 neuron with a sigmoid activation function and trained end-to-end, with a fixed learning rate of 10^{-5} for 150 epoches. Furthermore, the architecture is also used as a feature extraction network and a random forest classifier is trained to perform the classification, instead of the final fully-connected layer.

3.4   Classification Results

The results of the conducted classification experiments are summarised in Table 1 and Fig. 4. The architecture based uniquely on the spectrograms in combination with the deep learning architecture is outperformed by the other architectures in both experiments (left and right forearm). This can be explained by the limited size of the training data. The designed architecture is therefore not able to generate competitive discriminative features for the classification task, limiting its performance to 60.32% and 61.04%, for the left and right forearm respectively.

Table 1. Leave One User Out (LOUO) Cross Validation Evaluation (Mean(in %) ± Standard Deviation). The best performance is depicted in bold.

Forearm	Deep features	Hand-crafted features	Late fusion (Average Pooling)	Proposed approach (Dense)	Proposed approach (Random Forest)
Left	60.32 ± 11.87	61.33 ± 14.13	62.19 ± 13.85	$\mathbf{63.15 \pm 14.79}$	62.81 ± 15.49
Right	61.04 ± 14.58	64.16 ± 15.07	63.81 ± 15.93	64.65 ± 13.84	$\mathbf{65.63 \pm 13.62}$

Meanwhile, the proposed architecture outperforms the other classification architectures and is able to improve the performance of the system to a classification rate of 63.15% and 65.63% for the left and right forearm respectively. Since it also outperforms the late fusion approach, the network is able to exploit the information embedded in both spectrograms and hand-crafted features by training the whole architecture end-to-end, thus improving the classification performance. However, the limited amount of training samples hinders the generalisation ability of the deep architecture. It is believed that the performance of the proposed approach can be boosted by using more training data and optimising the regularisation approaches.

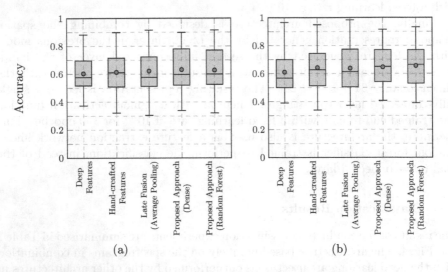

(a)   (b)

Fig. 4. Audio based Pain Intensity Classification Results (leave one user out cross validation evaluation). (a): Left Forearm. (b): Right Forearm. The mean and median classification accuracy across all 40 participants are depicted respectively with a dot and a horizontal line within each box plot.

4   Conclusion and Future Work

In this work, several combination approaches of hand-crafted features and deep features for pain classification based on breathing recordings have been assessed. This task has proven to be very challenging, since the experimental settings for the data acquisition did not include any type of verbal interaction, and the resulting training material consists of breathing and sporadic moaning sounds. The proposed classification approach, which consists of the combination of abstract representations generated by fully-connected layers with spatio-temporal representations generated by combined time-distributed CNN and bidirectional LSTM, has been able to outperform the other classification architectures. Still, the limited size of the training material hinders the overall performance of the deep learning architecture. Therefore, data augmentation methods and transfer learning approaches will be addressed in future iterations of the current work, in order to improve the performance as well as the robustness of the designed classification approach.

Acknowledgments. This paper is based on work done within the project *SenseEmotion* funded by the Federal Ministry of Education and Research (BMBF). We gratefully acknowledge the support of NVIDIA Corporation with the donation of the Tesla K40 GPU used for this research.

References

1. Abadi, M., et al.: Tensorflow: Large-scale Machine Learning on Heterogeneous Systems (2015). https://www.tensorflow.org/. Software available from tensorflow.org
2. Aung, M.S.H., et al.: The automatic detection of chronic pain-related expression: requirements, challenges and multimodal dataset. IEEE Trans. Affect. Comput. **7**(4), 435–451 (2016)
3. Breiman, L.: Random forests. Mach. Learn. **45**(1), 5–32 (2001)
4. Chen, Q., Zhang, W., Tian, X., Zhang, X., Chen, S., Lei, W.: Automatic heart and lung sounds classification using convolutional neural networks. In: 2016 Asia-Pacific Signal and Information Processing Association Annual Summit and Conference (APSIPA), pp. 1–4 (2016)
5. Chollet, F., et al.: Keras (2015). https://keras.io
6. Chu, Y., Zhao, X., Han, J., Su, Y.: Physiological signal-based method for measurement of pain intensity. Front Neurosci. **11**, 279 (2017)
7. Kingma, D.P., Ba, J.: Adam: a method for stochastic optimization. CoRR (2014)
8. Eyben, F., Weninger, F., Gross, F., Schuller, B.: Recent developments in openSMILE, the Munich open-source multimedia feature extractor. In: ACM Multimedia (MM), pp. 835–838 (2013)
9. Glodek, M., et al.: Fusion paradigms in cognitive technical systems for human-computer interaction. Neurocomputing **161**, 17–37 (2015)
10. Glodek, M., et al.: Multiple classifier systems for the classification of audio-visual emotional states. In: D'Mello, S., Graesser, A., Schuller, B., Martin, J.-C. (eds.) ACII 2011. LNCS, vol. 6975, pp. 359–368. Springer, Heidelberg (2011). https://doi.org/10.1007/978-3-642-24571-8_47
11. Hochreiter, S., Bengio, Y., Frasconi, P.: Gradient flow in recurrent nets: the difficulty of learning long-term dependencies. In: Field Guide to Dynamical Recurrent Networks. IEEE Press (2001)
12. Hochreiter, S., Schmidhuber, J.: Long short-term memory. Neural Comput. **9**(8), 1735–1780 (1997)
13. Kächele, M., et al.: Adaptive confidence learning for the personalization of pain intensity estimation systems. Evolv. Syst. **8**(1), 1–13 (2016)
14. Kächele, M., Schels, M., Meudt, S., Palm, G., Schwenker, F.: Revisiting the emotiw challenge: how wild is it really? J. Multimodal User In. **10**(2), 151–162 (2016)
15. Kächele, M., Thiam, P., Amirian, M., Schwenker, F., Palm, G.: Methods for person-centered continuous pain intensity assessment from bio-physiological channels. IEEE J. Sel. Top. Signal Process. **10**(5), 854–864 (2016)
16. Kessler, V., Thiam, P., Amirian, M., Schwenker, F.: Pain recognition with camera photoplethysmography. In: 2017 Seventh International Conference on Image Processing Theory, Tools and Applications (IPTA), pp. 1–5 (2017)
17. Kim, D.H., Baddar, W.J., Jang, J., Ro, Y.M.: Multi-objective based spatio-temporal feature representation learning robust to expression intensity variations for facial expression recognition. IEEE Trans. Affect. Comput. **1**, 1 (2017)

18. Kim, J., Truong, K.P., Englebienne, G., Evers, V.: Learning spectro-temporal features with 3D CNNs for speech emotion recognition. In: 2017 Seventh International Conference on Affective Computing and Intelligent Interaction (ACII), pp. 383–388 (2017)
19. Lim, W., Jang, D., Lee, T.: Speech emotion recognition using convolutional and recurrent neural networks. In: 2016 Asia-Pacific Signal and Information Processing Association Annual Summit and Conference (APSIPA), pp. 1–4 (2016)
20. Lucey, P., Cohn, J.F., Prkachin, K.M., Solomon, P.E., Matthews, I.: Painful data: the UNBC-McMaster shoulder pain expression archive database. In: Face and Gesture, pp. 57–64 (2011)
21. McFee, B., et al.: librosa: audio and music signal analysis in python. In: Proceedings of the 14th Python in Science Conference, pp. 18–25 (2015)
22. Pedregosa, F., et al.: Scikit-learn: machine learning in Python. J. Mach. Learn. Res. **12**, 2825–2830 (2011)
23. Rodriguez, P., et al.: Deep pain: exploiting long short-term memory networks for facial expression classification. IEEE Trans. Cybern., 1–11 (2017)
24. Srivastava, N., Hinton, G., Krizhevsky, A., Sutskever, I., Salakhutdinov, R.: Dropout: a simple way to prevent neural networks from overfitting. J. Mach. Learn. Res. **15**, 1929–1958 (2014)
25. Thiam, P., et al.: Multi-modal pain intensity recognition based on the SenseEmotion database. IEEE Trans. Affect. Comput., 1–11 (2019)
26. Thiam, P., Kessler, V., Walter, S., Palm, G., Schwenker, F.: Audio-visual recognition of pain intensity. In: Schwenker, F., Scherer, S. (eds.) MPRSS 2016. LNCS (LNAI), vol. 10183, pp. 110–126. Springer, Cham (2017). https://doi.org/10.1007/978-3-319-59259-6_10
27. Thiam, P., Schwenker, F.: Multi-modal data fusion for pain intensity assessement and classification. In: 2017 Seventh International Conference on Image Processing Theory, Tools and Applications (IPTA), pp. 1–6 (2017)
28. Trentin, E., Scherer, S., Schwenker, F.: Emotion recognition from speech signals via a probabilistic echo-state network. Pattern Recogn. Lett. **66**, 4–12 (2015)
29. Velana, M., et al.: The SenseEmotion database: a multimodal database for the development and systematic validation of an automatic pain- and emotion-recognition system. In: Schwenker, F., Scherer, S. (eds.) MPRSS 2016. LNCS (LNAI), vol. 10183, pp. 127–139. Springer, Cham (2017). https://doi.org/10.1007/978-3-319-59259-6_11
30. Walter, S., et al.: The BioVid heat pain database data for the advancement and systematic validation of an automated pain recognition system. In: 2013 IEEE International Conference on Cybernetics, pp. 128–131 (2013)
31. Werner, P., Al-Hamadi, A., Limbrecht-Ecklundt, K., Walter, S., Gruss, S., Traue, H.C.: Automatic pain assessment with facial activity descriptors. IEEE Trans. Affect. Comput. **8**(3), 286–299 (2017)
32. Yan, J., Zheng, W., Vui, Z., Song, P.: A joint convolutional bidirectional LSTM framework for facial expression recognition. IEICE Trans. Inf. Syst. **E101–D**, 1217–1220 (2018)

Deep Learning Algorithms for Emotion Recognition on Low Power Single Board Computers

Venkatesh Srinivasan, Sascha Meudt^(✉), and Friedhelm Schwenker

Institute of Neural Information Processing, Ulm University,
James Franck Ring, 89081 Ulm, Germany
{venkatesh.srinivasan,sascha.meudt,friedhelm.schwenker}@uni-ulm.de

Abstract. In the world of Human-Computer Interaction, a computer should have the ability to communicate with humans. One of the communication skill that a computer requires is to recognize the emotional state of the human. With the state-of-the-art computing systems along with Graphical Processing Units, a Deep Neural Network can be realized by training on any publicly available dataset and learn the whole emotion estimation into one single network. In a real-time application, the inference of such a network may not need high computational power as training a network does.

Several Single Board Computers (SBC) such as Raspberry Pi is now available with sufficient computational power wherein during inference; small Deep Neural Networks models could perform well enough with acceptable accuracy and processing delay. The paper deals in exploring SBC capabilities for DNN inference, where we prepare a target platform on which real-time camera sensor data is processed to detect face regions and succeed further with recognizing emotions. Several DNN architectures are evaluated on SBC considering processing delay, possible frame rates and classification accuracy on SBC. Finally, a Neural Compute Stick (NCS) such as Intel's Movidius is used to look at the performance of SBC for Emotion classification.

Keywords: Emotion Recognition · Deep Neural Networks · Single Board Computers

1 Introduction

Communication is of vital importance, whether it is a human or a machine [13]. While machines communicate through bits and bytes, humans can communicate in several ways such as speech, body gestures and facial expressions. Psychologically, emotions could be understood with the subjective experiences accompanied by physiological, behavioral and cognitive changes with reactions. Each emotion is distinctive in producing different patterns in brain activation signals. For example, considering an emotion with surprise, the heart rate in

F. Schwenker and S. Scherer (Eds.): MPRSS 2018, LNAI 11377, pp. 59–70, 2019.
https://doi.org/10.1007/978-3-030-20984-1_6

humans may be increased due to being startled, humans could also have our muscles being temporarily tensed and relaxed. The annotation of such signal is a complex task which can be supported by annotation tools and active learning algorithms [12,20]. In order to capture human emotions facial expressions is one of the methods to identify the existence of emotion, but there is always a possibility to combine speech recognition system to detect emotion or gesture-based emotion detection [7]. Such kind of human emotion detection system requires multimodal data which contains facial expressions, vocal expressions, body gestures, and physiological signals [15].

Thus, a complex system needs to be realized which often requires a high computation power [6,10,16]. Machine Learning applications are often dependent on several libraries that utilize multi-core architectures and hence reducing the overall processing time. Several machine learning libraries are officially supported for different architectures. In this paper, Raspberry PI (RPI) is chosen as SBC due to its low cost and low power architectures. Having 64 bit support to RPI would eventually allow us to have more addressing space and also different instruction set that could operate on 64-bit data. Hence there is need of 64-bit Linux operating system with several machine learning libraries supporting inferencing on ARMV8 architecture. Additionally, a DNN needs to be trained to extract features using Convolutional Neural Networks (CNN) for Facial Emotion Recognition (FER) classification on FER 2013 public dataset. Several DNN architectures are evaluated for inference. With the availability of NCS from Intel, evaluation is done for loading the neural network in the NCS using SBC as the host system.

Further sections of the paper are organized as follows: Sect. 2 provides a short literature survey on Emotion Recognition. Emotion Recognition System is described in Sect. 3. In Sect. 4, we discuss on results obtained for evaluating the dataset, feature map outputs, DNN models training and performance evaluation. Further discussion along with a live video output to detect emotions is visualized in Sect. 5. Finally, Sect. 6 concludes the paper with future work.

2   Background

Ekman et al. initially identified the basic emotion theory comprising of emotions that are constant across the cultures, and they are identified through facial expressions [3]. Fasel et al. have made an extensive survey on automatic facial expressions [4]. A framework for Facial expression analysis are discussed which consists of (1) Face Acquisition (2) Facial Feature Extraction and (3) Facial Expression Classification. Several methods that are available for each of these categories are well explained.

Haar-like features were proposed by Viola Jones for detecting faces [21]. Training of such a classifier takes more time because of the large dataset typically around 5000 faces and 35000 non-faces, but once trained, an inference of the face region is fast enough and also computation friendly when compared to several other methods such as deep convolution networks. Haar cascade methods are widely used in object detection [17].

An Emotion Recognition is proposed by Baveye et al. which is based on video dataset that is annotated version of 30 movies along the valence and arousal axis [2]. They use machine learning algorithms that are based on CNN, Support Vector Machines (SVM) for Regression and also a combination of both known as Transfer Learning. With the availability of powerful embedded systems, researchers are up in identifying the performance of CNN on embedded systems. Pena et al. have presented the benchmarking for networks namely GoogLeNet [18], AlexNet [8], Network in Network [24], CIFAR10 [11] on target devices RPI, Intel Joule 570X and also using a NCS [14].

A framework using deep cascaded multi-task is proposed by Zhang et al. where the model develops an inherent correlation and eventually boost the network performance [25]. The design consists of three cascaded CNN networks, where predictions are carried out in a coarse-to-fine manner. These networks are trained using WIDERFACE [23] dataset for face detection and Annotated Facial Landmarks in the Wild (AFLW) benchmarking for face alignment. Although this multi-task cascaded CNN is complex, it has proven to meet the real-time performance as well. Weighted Mixture Deep Neural Network (WMDNN) is used by fusing the weights from two different CNN, while the first DNN uses a VGG16 network that is trained on the ImageNet database and the other uses a shallow CNN [22].

With all the advancement in CNN's and DNN's, it is clear that the objective of using these networks are tending towards real-time processing using devices such as the Internet of Things (IoT), SBC, etc., Since these devices are low powered, additional add-on devices are being designed for processing huge DNN networks. Research is towards optimizing the hardware to make CNN's being used on low power hardware chips. Andri et al. provide a hardware accelerator specifically optimized for binary weighted CNN's [1]. The usage of CNN's during training addresses the need for removing extensive computations by limiting to binary weights, resulting in reduced bandwidth and storage.

3 Emotion Recognition System

Emotion Recognition System consists of three phases:

- Face Detection
- Emotion Feature Extraction
- Emotion Classifier.

During the Face Recognition phase, a bounding box of the detected face is obtained first. To obtain a bounding box, two approaches have been used, Multi-Task Cascaded convolutional Neural Network (MTCNN) and Haar Cascade method. Once the bounding box is acquired in the image, the face region is cropped and resized to DNN input size, i.e., 48 × 48 pixels. Since a DNN of multiple layers is used, Emotion Feature Extraction and Emotion Classifier are combined, and the output of the Emotion Recognition DNN is the classifier output which has the probability estimation of emotions.

3.1 Deep Neural Networks

FER 2013 Database. As part of ICML challenge in 2013 [5], facial expression recognition database was introduced that was created using a search engine provided by Google, which is part of "In the wild" methodology of creating the database. The dataset was prepared by Pierre Luc Carrier and Aron Courville. In total, there are 35,887 images provided in the CSV file with the data columns consisting of Emotion Type, 1-D Grayscale image of dimension 48 × 48 and Image to be used for Training, Public (Validation) or Private (Testing) respectively.

Figure 1 shows the dataset distribution for 7 Emotions. We see an imbalanced dataset distribution for all the emotions. For example, Disgust emotion has the least number of data samples while Happy emotion has significantly more data samples. Overall, the distribution with other emotions except Disgust and Happy seems to be reasonably distributed.

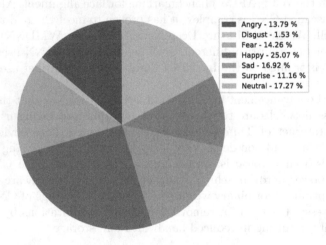

Fig. 1. FER2013 dataset distribution for 7 emotions

Models. The input images are of size 48 × 48 pixels that are single channel as they are grayscale. The DNN model consists of several CNN layers, Pooling layers, and Fully Connected (FC) layers. The kernel filter size plays a crucial role in computation complexity, and hence its size should be as minimal as possible. By using cascading of convolutional layers, it facilitates the model to learn more features but also keep the filter size minimal. We use Keras [9] as a machine learning API that uses TensorFlow [19] for model definition and training. A summary of models along with the number of parameters required for training is shown in Table 1.

To begin with, the model is designed to have a low number of features so that it gets trained to features such as lines and edges, and slowly the feature size keeps increasing. As an example, Fig. 2 shows the DNN architecture for all variants of ER DNN models. The input to the network is a 48 × 48 grayscale

Table 1. Training Model and its parameter count

Model name	Convolution layers	Pooling layers	Parameters
ermodel_cls7_conv3	3	2	5,036,775
ermodel_cls7_conv5	5	3	3,677,127
ermodel_cls7_conv8	8	4	2,826,759
ermodel_cls7_conv11	11	5	4,317,543
ermodel_cls7_conv13	13	5	6,595,655

image, a convolution layer with kernel size 3 × 3 is used along with Rectilinear Unit Function (ReLU) Activation, Max pooling of 2 × 2 size is used and padding as 'same'. The final block is a fully connected layer that has two 1024 Unit Dense layers, and the last layer of the model output is the classification output of 7 different classes that consist the probability estimate of each emotion class.

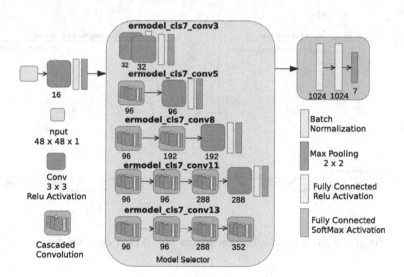

Fig. 2. Emotion Recognition DNN Model: Feature extraction and classification based on CNN

4 Results

4.1 Dataset Validation Results

Model evaluation and Model selection are the two factors that could be considered for dataset validation. The model selection consists of hyper-parameter tuning for a specific class of models such as neural networks, linear models, etc., and model evaluation finds the estimate of the predictive power for a specific model which is unbiased.

Figure 3 shows the 10-Fold cross-validation result for the neural network model shown in Fig. 2 which is an 11-CNN layer network. The mean value of the accuracy was 67.05%. As the standard deviation was 0.006 (0.6%), the test error that occurs during inference would be ±0.6%.

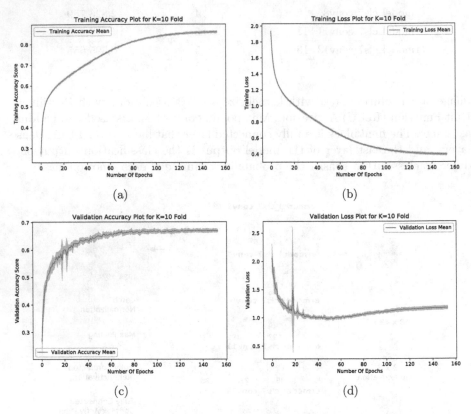

(a)   (b)

(c)   (d)

Fig. 3. Training and Validation results for 10-Fold cross validation

4.2   Feature Map Output

The feature maps that the DNN was trained can be visualized as shown in Fig. 4. To get these visualizations, an image of emotion "Happy" was given as input to *ermodel_cls7_conv3* network model which successfully classified the image as "Happy". For convolutional layers, the feature maps are the outputs of ReLU activation; the maps are shown in the figure represents a color map distribution of ReLU output for convolutional layer 1, 2 and 3. The ReLU functions activity could be visualized in the graph where a minimum value of zero is indicated with navy blue color and maximum value with yellow color. We could see that the DNN first learns to detect edges and slowly adapts to learn more detailed features.

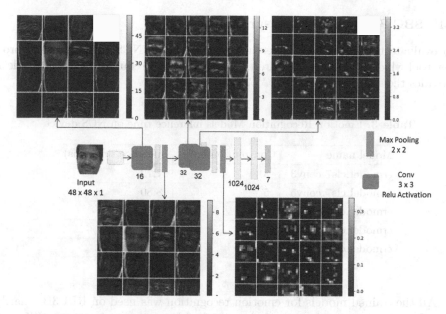

Fig. 4. Feature Map Outputs at several layers for *ermodel_cls7_conv3*

4.3   DNN Models Training

Emotion Recognition models were trained using FER2013 dataset. There were five network models each configured with an increasing size of convolution layers as shown in Table 1. The model name can be interpreted as *ermodel* - Emotion Recognition Model with *cls7* as number of emotion classifications and *convX* representing *X* layers of convolution in the model. A summary of training results for those networks is shown in Table 2. The accuracy for *ermodel_cls7_conv11* for Test dataset was 69% with train accuracy of 95.28% and is the highest among all the networks with 4,317,543 parameter count. *ermodel_cls_conv8* has the lowest parameters to be trained, i.e., 2,826,759, having an accuracy of 90.73% and 67.9% on the Training dataset and Test dataset respectively.

Table 2. Emotion Recognition Models with accuracies for Train, Validation and Test dataset for FER2013

Model name	Convolution layers	Epoch	Training accuracy (%)	Validation accuracy (%)	Testing accuracy (%)
ermodel_cls7_conv3	3	138	61.57	58.53	62.0
ermodel_cls7_conv5	5	302	74.18	65.89	66.9
ermodel_cls7_conv8	8	494	90.73	66.53	67.9
ermodel_cls7_conv11	11	483	95.28	66.75	69.0
ermodel_cls7_conv13	13	406	94.50	67.79	68.6

4.4 SBC Performance Measurements

To evaluate the ER models inference time on NCS, NCSDK provides a pro-filer tool which is used to measure the inference time required by NCS. Table 3 provides the summary of the *mvNCProfile* tool output.

Table 3. Emotion Recognition Models inference time on NCS device

Model name	Convolution layers	Inference time (ms)
ermodel_cls7_conv3	3	7.72
ermodel_cls7_conv5	5	8.80
ermodel_cls7_conv8	8	12.07
ermodel_cls7_conv11	11	16.07
ermodel_cls7_conv13	13	19.37

All the trained models for emotion recognition was used on RPI 3B+ hardware for detecting emotions through a live feed from camera interface. Different hardware configurations were used to evaluate four parameters:

- CPU Load: This metric is used to evaluate the RPI CPU in executing the DNN network for inference, and any I/O operations involving frame read from the camera, loading the DNN to NCS, etc.
- DNN Load Time: This metric is used to evaluate the initialization time of the application that involves loading of DNN libraries and also the Emotion Recognition model.
- Frame Rate: This metric is a measure of RPI capability to process the live feed images from the camera in one second.
- Processing Time: This metric provides the measure of time taken to process a single image captured from camera which includes reading the camera image, face region detection (RPI/NCS), emotion recognition inference (RPI/NCS) and displaying emotion graph in the Application GUI.

Figure 5(a)–(d) shows the plot of the above metrics. ER model inference is carried out using NCS and RPI, Face detection using Haar Cascade method is done using RPI, but while using MTCNN both RPI and also NCS (dual) are used.

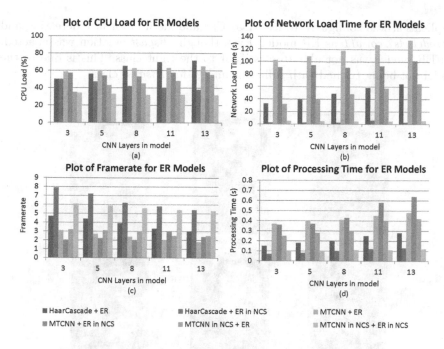

Fig. 5. Performance parameters measured on RPI and NCS

5   Discussion

As there are several configurations in which the ER could be run successfully for detecting emotions, some of the configurations come with the price
of cost and computation. In case of total price being the limitation, then ER
system could be completely run on RPI and in this case, using Haar Cascade method for face detection would be the best solution as it gives 4.5 fps
with a detection rate of 222 ms. To get an excellent fps and a detection rate
of 100 ms then using NCS would be more appropriate. Again in this configuration, Haar Cascade on RPI and ER on NCS has given a frame rate of
8 fps. Although the *ermodel_cls7_conv3* gives good frame rate, it would be better to use *ermodel_cls7_conv8* or *ermodel_cls7_conv11*, as it has shown better
accuracy in detecting emotions during live video feed testing. Furthermore,
ermodel_cls7_conv8 has less number of trained parameters and hence lower computation power and processing time. Furthermore, with the DNN models completely running on NCS, has a very low CPU usage, has not only stable processing time and loading time but also independent of ER models with a stable
frame rate between 5 to 6 fps. The overall system with this configuration would
be expensive to realize as it requires more NCS devices and could also lead to
communication overhead.

Figure 6 shows the ER graph for *Angry, Fear, Happy, Sad, Surprise* and
Neutral. Two different subjects were asked to enact several emotions and the ER

Application was configured to use Haar Cascade method for face detection and *ermodel_cls7_conv11* as ER model. Even though *Disgust* emotion was enacted, the ER model was not able to classify it to the right class. This is due to the model not being trained with sufficient images for *Disgust* class.

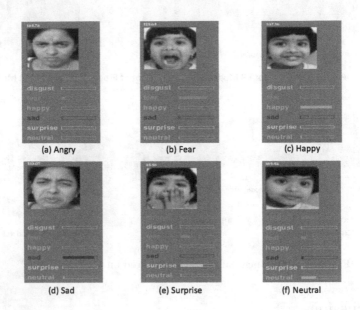

Fig. 6. ER Application showing ER graph of six basic emotions

6   Conclusion

Emotion Recognition System was realized on a SBC that could run on low power requirements. The system is used to recognize emotions through a live video interface that could successfully detect face regions and also predict the emotions. The work carried out required a Linux Operating system supporting ARMV8 on RPI so that the libraries required for DNN inference could be loaded successfully into SBC. Furthermore, the application used as a graphical user interface to display camera feed and emotion graph was designed using multi-threading concepts and hence utilizing the SBC multi-core architecture. By using CNN, several DNN architectures was realized to extract the features from the desired FER dataset. The CNN feature maps reveal the learned features in several CNN layers that were used for the classifier which was a simple MLP.

The choice of RPI for an SBC has proven to have sufficient CPU computation power for running the DNN algorithms. Results show that multiple DNN algorithms such as MTCNN and ER could perform well enough with a frame rate of around 2 fps on RPI. Given the fact that the change in emotions is not that instant in real-world applications, the frame rates achieved for all the configurations and ER DNN models are within the acceptable range. Furthermore, the best test accuracy achieved for FER2013 dataset was around 69% for *ermodel_cls7_conv11* ER model. The 10-Fold CV result for the model was with mean accuracy 67.05% ± 0.6% which indicates that the model is quite stable.

References

1. Andri, R., Cavigelli, L., Rossi, D., Benini, L.: Yoda NN: an architecture for ultralow power binary-weight CNN acceleration. IEEE Trans. Comput.-Aided Des. Integr. Circ. Syst. **37**(1), 48–60 (2018). https://doi.org/10.1109/TCAD.2017. 2682138. http://ieeexplore.ieee.org/document/7878541/

2. Baveye, Y., Dellandrea, E., Chamaret, C., Chen, L.: Deep learning vs. kernel methods: performance for emotion prediction in videos. In: 2015 International Conference on Affective Computing and Intelligent Interaction, ACII 2015, pp. 77–83. IEEE, September 2015. https://doi.org/10.1109/ACII.2015.7344554. http://ieeexplore.ieee.org/document/7344554/

3. Ekman, P., Friesen, W.V.: Constants across cultures in the face and emotion. J. Pers. Soc. Psychol. **17**(2), 124–129 (1971). https://doi.org/10.1037/h0030377

4. Fasel, B., Luettin, J.: Automatic facial expression analysis: a survey. Pattern Recognit. **36**(1), 259–275 (2003)

5. Goodfellow, I.J., et al.: Challenges in representation learning: a report on three machine learning contests. Neural Netw. **64**, 59–63 (2015). https://doi.org/10. 1016/j.neunet.2014.09.005

6. Kächele, M., Glodek, M., Zharkov, D., Meudt, S., Schwenker, F.: Fusion of audiovisual features using hierarchical classifier systems for the recognition of affective states and the state of depression. Depression **1**(1) (2014)

7. Kächele, M., Schels, M., Meudt, S., Palm, G., Schwenker, F.: Revisiting the emotiw challenge: how wild is it really? J. Multimodal User Interfaces **10**(2), 151–162 (2016)

8. Kalash, M., Rochan, M., Mohammed, N., Bruce, N.D., Wang, Y., Iqbal, F.: Malware classification with deep convolutional neural networks. In: 2018 9th IFIP International Conference on New Technologies, Mobility and Security, NTMS 2018 - Proceedings, January 2018, pp. 1–5 (2018). https://doi.org/10.1109/NTMS.2018. 8328749

9. Keras: The Python Deep Learning Library. https://keras.io/. Accessed 08 Dec 2018

10. Kindsvater, D., Meudt, S., Schwenker, F.: Fusion architectures for multimodal cognitive load recognition. In: Schwenker, F., Scherer, S. (eds.) MPRSS 2016. LNCS (LNAI), vol. 10183, pp. 36–47. Springer, Cham (2017). https://doi.org/10.1007/ 978-3-319-59259-6_4

11. Krizhevsky, A., Hinton, G.E.: Convolutional deep belief networks on CIFAR-10, pp. 1–9 (2010, unpublished manuscript)

12. Meudt, S., Bigalke, L., Schwenker, F.: Atlas-annotation tool using partially supervised learning and multi-view co-learning in human-computer-interaction scenarios. In: 2012 11th International Conference on Information Science, Signal Processing and their Applications (ISSPA), pp. 1309–1312. IEEE (2012)

13. Meudt, S., et al.: Going further in affective computing: how emotion recognition can improve adaptive user interaction. In: Esposito, A., Jain, L.C. (eds.) Toward Robotic Socially Believable Behaving Systems - Volume I. ISRL, vol. 105, pp. 73–103. Springer, Cham (2016). https://doi.org/10.1007/978-3-319-31056-5_6

14. Pena, D., Forembski, A., Xu, X., Moloney, D.: Benchmarking of CNNs for low-cost, low-power robotics applications. In: RSS 2017 Workshop: New Frontier for Deep Learning in Robotics, pp. 1–5 (2017)
15. Schwenker, F., et al.: Multimodal affect recognition in the context of human-computer interaction for *companion*-systems. In: Biundo, S., Wendemuth, A. (eds.) Companion Technology. CT, pp. 387–408. Springer, Cham (2017). https://doi.org/10.1007/978-3-319-43665-4_19
16. Siegert, I., et al.: Multi-modal information processing in *companion*-systems: a ticket purchase system. In: Biundo, S., Wendemuth, A. (eds.) Companion Technology. CT, pp. 493–500. Springer, Cham (2017). https://doi.org/10.1007/978-3-319-43665-4_25
17. Soo, S.: Object detection using Haar-cascade Classifier. Inst. Comput. Sci. Univ. Tartu **2**(3), 1–12 (2014)
18. Szegedy, C., et al.: Going deeper with convolutions. In: Proceedings of the IEEE Computer Society Conference on Computer Vision and Pattern Recognition, vol. 07, pp. 1–9, 12 June 2015. https://doi.org/10.1109/CVPR.2015.7298594
19. TensorFlow: An Open Source Machine Learning Framework for Everyone. https://www.tensorflow.org/. Accessed 08 Dec 2018
20. Thiam, P., Meudt, S., Palm, G., Schwenker, F.: A temporal dependency based multi-modal active learning approach for audiovisual event detection. Neural Process. Lett. **48**(2), 709–732 (2018)
21. Viola, P., Jones, M.: Rapid object detection using a boosted cascade of simple features. In: Proceedings of the 2001 IEEE Computer Society Conference on Computer Vision and Pattern Recognition, CVPR 2001, vol. 1, pp. I-511–I-518. IEEE Computer Society (2001). https://doi.org/10.1109/CVPR.2001.990517. http://ieeexplore.ieee.org/document/990517/
22. Yang, B., Cao, J., Ni, R., Zhang, Y.: Facial expression recognition using weighted mixture deep neural network based on double-channel facial images. IEEE Access **6**, 4630–4640 (2017). https://doi.org/10.1109/ACCESS.2017.2784096
23. Yang, S., Luo, P., Loy, C.C., Tang, X.: WIDER FACE: a face detection benchmark. In: 2016 IEEE Conference on Computer Vision and Pattern Recognition (CVPR), pp. 5525–5533. IEEE, June 2016. https://doi.org/10.1109/CVPR.2016.596. http://ieeexplore.ieee.org/document/7780965/
24. Yoshioka, T., et al.: The NTT CHiME-3 system: advances in speech enhancement and recognition for mobile multi-microphone devices. In: 2015 IEEE Workshop on Automatic Speech Recognition and Understanding (ASRU), pp. 436–443. IEEE, December 2015. https://doi.org/10.1109/ASRU.2015.7404828. http://ieeexplore.ieee.org/document/7404828/
25. Zhang, K., Zhang, Z., Li, Z., Qiao, Y.: Joint face detection and alignment using multitask cascaded convolutional networks. IEEE Signal Process. Lett. **23**(10), 1499–1503 (2016). https://doi.org/10.1109/LSP.2016.2603342. http://ieeexplore.ieee.org/document/7553523/

Improving Audio-Visual Speech Recognition Using Gabor Recurrent Neural Networks

Ali S. Saudi[1], Mahmoud I. Khalil[2], and Hazem M. Abbas[2(✉)]

[1] Faculty of Media Engineering and Technology,
German University in Cairo, New Cairo, Egypt
ali.saudi@guc.edu.eg
[2] Faculty of Engineering, Ain Shams University, Cairo, Egypt
{mahmoud.khalil,hazem.abbas}@eng.asu.edu.eg

Abstract. The performance of speech recognition systems can be significantly improved when visual information is used in conjunction with the audio ones, especially in noisy environments. Prompted by the great achievements of deep learning in solving Audio-Visual Speech Recognition (AVSR) problems, we propose a deep AVSR model based on Long Short-Term Memory Bidirectional Recurrent Neural Network (LSTM-BRNN). The proposed deep AVSR model utilizes the Gabor filters in both the audio and visual front-ends with Early Integration (EI) scheme. This model is termed as $BRNN_{av}$ model. The Gabor features simulate the underlying spatiotemporal processing chain that occurs in the Primary Audio Cortex (PAC) in conjunction with Primary Visual Cortex (PVC). We named it Gabor Audio Features (GAF) and Gabor Visual Features (GVF). The experimental results show that the deep Gabor (LSTM-BRNNs)-based model achieves superior performance when compared to the (GMM-HMM)-based models which utilize the same front-ends. Furthermore, the use of GAF and GVF in both audio and visual front-ends attain significant improvement in the performance compared to the traditional audio and visual features.

Keywords: Audio-Visual Speech Recognition ·
Bidirectional Recurrent Neural Network · Gabor filters

1 Introduction

The human brain can recognize speech by correlating the audio data (or phonemes) with visual data coming from lip movements (or visemes). McGurk's effect [9] has proven this audio-visual relationship, where the voicing of /ba-ba/ with lip movements of /ga-ga/ will be translated into the brain as /da-da/. In contrast to this effect when there is an acoustic noise, it is easier to understand what someone is saying when you can see and follow their lip motions. The visual modality which carries complementary information is actually very

© Springer Nature Switzerland AG 2019
F. Schwenker and S. Scherer (Eds.): MPRSS 2018, LNAI 11377, pp. 71–83, 2019.
https://doi.org/10.1007/978-3-030-20984-1_7

useful in improving the accuracy of speech recognition, especially in noisy and reverberant environments [15].

Deep Neural Networks (DNNs) have been applied to solve several speech recognition problems whether Audio-only (ASR) [13], Visual-only (VSR) [15,16] or Audio-Visual Speech Recognition (AVSR) [2,13,18]. The use of various DNNs-based systems not only improved the recognition performance but also introduced a new level of robustness against noise, compared to traditional Gaussian Mixture Model-Hidden Markov Model (GMM-HMM)-based systems.

The process of selecting and extracting the sensory information is crucial as it affects the overall system performance. In this work, the spectral-temporal features correspond to the audio-visual signals nature. Physiologically, the Primary Audio Cortex (PAC) and Primary Visual Cortex (PVC) are two processing units in the human brain that extract the auditory and visual information [8,10,11]. The neuronal responses in both PAC and PVC can discriminate small changes in the spectro-temporal representation of the signal [10]. The estimation of this representation that stimuli the neuronal response is called the Spectro-Temporal Receptive Field (STRF).

In this paper, a deep AVSR model based on Long Short-Term Memory Bidirectional Recurrent Neural Network (LSTM-BRNN) is introduced. The proposed deep AVSR model utilizes the Gabor filters in both the audio and visual frontends with Early Integration (EI) scheme. We named it Gabor Audio Features (GAF) and Gabor Visual Features (GVF). First, we propose two LSTM-BRNN networks: one for ASR and the other for VSR, given the names $BRNN_a$ and $BRNN_v$, to model the sequential characteristics of each modality separately. Second, an audio-visual network that models the multimodal EI scheme of both modalities, named as $BRNN_{av}$ is introduced. Gabor filters are incorporated in all BRNN networks; the $BRNN_a$, $BRNN_v$, and $BRNN_{av}$. The GAF and GVF are fed separately to the $BRNN_a$, $BRNN_v$, and a fused version of both Gabor features (GAF and GVF) is fed to the $BRNN_{av}$ network. The performance obtained after feeding the BRNNs with the proposed Gabor features is compared to the performance obtained after feeding the same networks with the traditional audio, visual, and fused audio-visual features MFCC, DCT, and (MFCC and DCT), respectively. In addition, we compare the performance of the proposed Gabor (LSTM-BRNNs)-based models with the traditional (GMM-HMM)-based models which use the same front-end. All of these models were trained and tested using clean and noisy recordings from Clemson University Audio Visual Experiment (CUAVE) corpus [14].

This paper is organized as follows: Sect. 2 provides background on Gabor filters as well as the different types of RNNs and its training using the Connectionist Temporal Classification (CTC) function. Section 3 explains how the EI scheme takes place in the proposed AVSR systems. Section 4 discusses our audio-visual corpus and reports experimental results. Finally, Sect. 5 presents conclusions and future work.

2   Related Work

This section provides a brief review of Gabor filters and how they can be employed in several deep learning architectures to solve many problems in the literature. Furthermore, the section reviews the RNNs types and utilization of RNNs in solving the uni-modal and multi-modal problems and its training using the CTC loss function.

2.1   Gabor Filters

Gabor filters, named after Dennis Gabor [3], have been employed to model the STRF that stimuli the neuronal response in both PAC [1] and PVC [8,11].

The Gabor filter $\Psi_{u,v}(z)$ of orientation v and size u is defined as follows [20]:

$$\Psi_{u,v}(z) = \frac{||k_{u,v}||^2}{\sigma^2} e^{-(||k_{u,v}||^2||z||^2/2\sigma^2)} [e^{ik_{u,v}z} - e^{-\sigma^2/2}] \tag{1}$$

where $z = (x, y)$, $k_{u,v} = k_v e^{ik_u}$, $k_v = (\pi/2)/\sqrt{2}^{(v-1)}$, $k_u = u\frac{\pi}{U}$, with $v = 0, ..., V$ and $u = 0, ..., U$ and v is the frequency and u is the orientation, and $\sigma = 2\pi$. GAF and GVF are computed using filtering process of the input $I(z)$ with the Gabor filter $\Psi_{u,v}(z)$ [17]:

$$G_{u,v}(z) = I(z) * \Psi_{u,v}(z) \tag{2}$$

where $I(z) = \{I_a(z), I_v(z)\}$ denote the 25 ms speech frame $I_a(z)$ or the mouth ROI image $I_v(z)$, and $G_{u,v}(z)$ represents the filtering output.

2.2   Recurrent Neural Networks

RNNs are very powerful models in solving problems that require sequences of data similar to speech recognition and machine translation [2]. They successfully have been employed to solve many uni-modal and multi-modal speech recognition problems, such as ASR [6], VSR [15,16], and AVSR [2,18].

RNNs have a memory that retains information about what has already been computed so far to be used in forthcoming decisions. So, the output is, not only, dependent on the current (or present) input, but also on what it has learned from the previously received input (or recent past) which was saved in its memory. Figure 1 illustrates the standard RNN model where the hidden layer output cycles through a loop. By unfolding (or unrolling) this loop, as shown on the network on the right, it means that we can feed the RNN with a complete sequence of data.

Assuming that the input, hidden and output layer at time t are denoted by $x^{(t)}$, $h^{(t)}$, and $o^{(t)}$, respectively. The prediction of the output $o^{(t)}$ can be computed as follows [2]:

$$\begin{aligned} a^{(t)} &= b_1 + Wh^{(t-1)} + Ux^{(t)} \\ h^{(t)} &= \sigma(a^{(t)}) \\ o^{(t)} &= b_2 + Vh^{(t)} \end{aligned} \tag{3}$$

Where U, V, and W are the RNN weighting parameters (or matrices); b_1 and b_2 are bias vectors; and σ is the sigmoid activation function $\sigma(x) = (1 + e^{-x})^{-1}$.

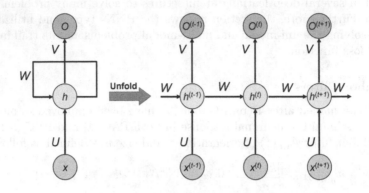

Fig. 1. The standard RNN and the unfolding in time.

The bidirectional RNN (BRNN) is an extension to the standard RNN, where two independent RNNs are stacked above each other. The input stream is fed forward in time for one network to learn from the previous calculations; and backward in time for another to learn from the future calculations. In this case, the output depends on three elements: the present, the recent past, and the future elements. Figure 2 illustrates the typical structure of the BRNN.

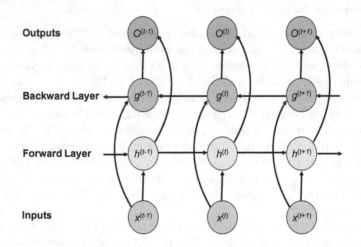

Fig. 2. The BRNN structure.

When the time steps increase, RNNs training will be vulnerable to the vanishing or exploding back-propagation gradient problem. To resolve this problem,

Hochreiter and Schmidhuber proposed LSTM networks which enable the RNNs to learn long-term dependencies [7]. LSTM networks store their information in a set of gated memory cells. Each memory cell has three gates: one that determines whether the new information will be stored in the cell or not (input gate), the other gate decides whether the cell content will be cleared or not (forget gate), and the last gate decides whether to allow the cell content to affect the output in the current time step or not (output gate).

2.3 Connectionist Temporal Classification

BRNNs utilized in speech recognizers are frame-level classifiers. A proper alignment between the audio and transcription sequences at each frame is required during the BRNNs training phase. The CTC [4,5] is an objective loss function that can resolve such explicit problem as it allows the BRNNs to be trained over all possible input-output alignments. In the same way, the CTC objective function is utilized to align a sequence of mouth images into transcription sequences in VSR systems.

Assume that the audio-only and visual-only feature vectors of length T are denoted by $\mathbf{X}_a = (\overline{X}_{a,1}, \overline{X}_{a,2}, ..., \overline{X}_{a,T})$ and $\mathbf{X}_v = (\overline{X}_{v,1}, \overline{X}_{v,2}, ..., \overline{X}_{v,T})$ where $\overline{X}_{a,t} \in \mathbb{R}^{d_a}$ and $\overline{X}_{v,t} \in \mathbb{R}^{d_v}$. To ensure equal frame rates, the visual features rate is up-sampled to reach the audio frame rate using linear interpolation. $\mathbf{X}_{av} = (\overline{X}_{av,1}, \overline{X}_{av,2}, ..., \overline{X}_{av,T})$ where $\overline{X}_{av,t} = [\overline{X}_{a,t}, \overline{X}_{v,t}] \in \mathbb{R}^{d_{av}}$ where $d_{av} = d_a + d_v$ is the concatenated audio-visual feature vector at time t.

The corresponding transcription sequence $\mathbf{l} = (l_1, l_2, ..., l_S)$ where $S \leq T$ and $l_i \in L$ where L is the English alphabets set plus an extra symbol referred to as the blank token ϕ representing a null emission. The BRNN utilizes a softmax output layer containing one unit for each element in L' where $L' = L \cup \{\phi\}$.

Generally, let $\mathbf{X} = (\overline{X}_1, \overline{X}_2, ..., \overline{X}_T)$ denotes an input sequence $\mathbf{X}$ of length T. The probability of emitting a label (or a blank token) with index $c \in L'$ at time t is calculated using the softmax function as follows [4]:

$$P(c_t|\overline{X}_t) = \frac{\exp(y_t^c)}{\sum_{c'} \exp(y_t^{c'})} \tag{4}$$

where y_t^c is element c of the softmax layer at time t. The labels are conditionally independent at each time index (like HMMs). A CTC alignment π is a length T sequence containing elements of L'. The probability $P(\pi|\mathbf{X})$ is modeled by the product of the label emission probabilities at every time-step [4]:

$$P(\pi|\mathbf{X}) = \prod_{t=1}^{T} P(c_t|\overline{X}_t) \tag{5}$$

There are many possible alignments for a given transcription sequence. For example, $(z, \phi, e, \phi, r, o, \phi, \phi)$, $(\phi, z, \phi, e, \phi, r, \phi, o)$, (z, e, e, e, r, r, o), and $(z, \phi, e, \phi, r, o, o)$ are different alignments of length eight correspond to the transcription sequence (z, e, r, o).

A many-to-one map operator $\beta : L' \longmapsto L^{\leq T}$ is defined to generate a transcription sequence by removing all repeated blanks and labels from an alignment. Given an input sequence $\mathbf{X}$, the likelihood of the transcription sequence $\mathbf{l} \in L'$ is equal to the sum of the probabilities of all possible alignments corresponding to it [4]:

$$P(\mathbf{l}|\mathbf{X}) = \sum_{\pi \in \beta^{-1}(\mathbf{l})} P(\pi|\mathbf{X}) \qquad (6)$$

Finally, the BRNN network can be trained to minimize the negative log-likelihood of the target transcription sequence $\mathbf{l}^*$ as follows [4]:

$$\mathcal{L}_{CTC}(\mathbf{X}, \mathbf{l}^*) = -\log P(\mathbf{l}^*|\mathbf{X}) \qquad (7)$$

3 Integration Models

The features from different modalities have to be integrated at a particular level. There are two schemes to deal with different types of features, the EI and Late Integration (LI) [12]. In this paper, we apply the EI scheme on the HMM-based and deep BRNN-based models which utilize the same audio-visual features. In the EI scheme, the audio and visual features are concatenated or fused together to form a single feature vector. The fused audio-visual feature vector is used to train/test a single-stream HMM_{av} and a single deep BRNN_{av} AVSR models.

3.1 Single-Stream HMM_{av} AVSR Model Setup

The structure of the HMM classifier that used in all experiments; ASR, VSR, and AVSR experiments, is the traditional single-stream HMM model. In all HMM experiments, we employed left-to-right topology with a varying number of states, from three to fifteen states, with one-GMM per state. The models are trained using the Baum-Welch algorithm that employs the Expectation-Maximization (EM) algorithm to get the Maximum Likelihood Estimate (MLE) of the HMM parameter set. The HMM Toolkit (HTK) is used for the training and testing phases.

Given the fused feature vector $\overline{X}_{av,t}$, the state/class emission probability of the single-stream HMM_{av} AVSR model is given by [13]:

$$P_{av}(\overline{X}_{av,t}|c) = \sum_{j=1}^{J_c} \omega_{cj} \mathcal{N}(\overline{X}_{av,t}, m_{cj}, v_{cj}) \qquad (8)$$

where $c \in L'$ is the class indicator, J_c is the number of Gaussian components for class c, ω_{cj} is the mixture weights for j^{th} Gaussian mixture component which are positive numbers that their summation is equal to one, and finally m_{cj} and v_{cj} represent the mean and the variance values of the Gaussian component. Figure 3 shows the structure of the single-stream HMM_{av} AVSR model.

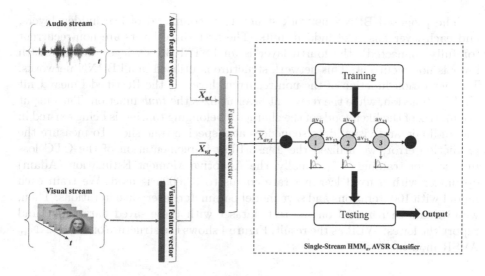

Fig. 3. The proposed HMM*av* AVSR model structure.

3.2   Deep BRNN$_{av}$ AVSR Model Setup

The proposed deep BRNN models; BRNN$_a$, BRNN$_v$, and BRNN$_{av}$, utilize the same network structure with the same settings except for the feature type and feature vector size. We present a deep network structure which is based on the End-to-End acoustic model proposed by Hannun et al. [6] to solve the audio-only speech recognition problem using spectrograms as input audio features. On the other side, this paper modifies the audio-only model's structure proposed by [6] to develop and train other uni-modal models; BRNN$_a$ ASR and BRNN$_v$ VSR. That can be done through utilizing the Gabor filters to capture robust spectro-temporal features in both audio and visual front-ends. Moreover, this work extends the work in [6] to develop a multi-modal model; BRNN$_{av}$ AVSR, by extracting the visual information and fusing them with the audio ones.

The most common problem in the previous work regarding DNN is that there is not a clear determination of all the hyperparameters values. Sometimes these values are not even indicated at all. Determining a proper set of values for the hyperparameters of a DNN requires too much time of fine-tuning. These hyperparameters are the feature type (audio, visual, audio-visual), the feature vector size, the number of units in the hidden layers, the dropout rate for each layer, the learning rate, the network weights, the number of epochs, the number of elements in the training, validation, and testing batches. The main aim of the fine-tuning process of the hyperparameters is to find a robust model that achieves the minimum Word Error Rate (WER) results. The chosen hyperparameters values in this work (through a blend of intuition and haphazardness) were not the same to values chosen by the approach in [6], most likely because of little contrasts in the structure. For example, we utilized LSTM cells instead of Gated Repetitive Unit (GRU) cells in the BRNN layer.

The proposed BRNN network structure is composed of five hidden layers, and each layer has 1024 hidden units. The first three layers are non-recurrent (or fully connected), the fourth layer is an LSTM-BRNN layer, and the fifth layer is non-recurrent. This network structure is utilized in all BRNN networks. The activation function of the non-recurrent layers is the Rectified Linear Unit (ReLU) function, while the recurrent layer utilizes the *tanh* function. The output is a matrix of the likelihoods of the character belonging to what is being existed in the audio or/and visual data sequences at a specific time slice. To measure the prediction error, we utilized the TensorFlow implementation of the CTC loss function for training [4,5]. Finally, the Adaptive Moment Estimation (Adam) optimizer with a fixed learning rate equals to 0.00095 is used. We train each model with 100 iterations and save model parameters every five iterations. Then, we evaluate each model on the test dataset with these saved parameters and report the lowest WER as the result. Figure 4 shows the structure of the $BRNN_{av}$ AVSR model.

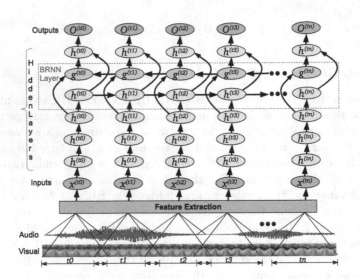

Fig. 4. The proposed $BRNN_{av}$ AVSR model structure.

4   Experimental Results

4.1   Data Corpus

We evaluated our simulation on the CUAVE benchmark [14]. It contains 36 speakers, nineteen male, and seventeen female uttering five repetitions of the continuous and isolated digits. To simulate audio degradation, the clean audio recordings were corrupted with additive white Gaussian noise from the NOISEX-92 collection at various SNR levels ranging from $-10\,dB$ to $20\,dB$ in steps of $5\,dB$. All models were trained and tested using the clean and noisy samples, so the total number of samples is 14400. The training, validation, and test set composed of 12000, 1200, and 1200 samples, respectively.

For the audio front-end, the traditional 26-MFCCs or the first 90-GAF were utilized as audio features. For the visual front-end, the Viola-Jones algorithm [19] is applied to 2D images twice. First, to detect the subject's face and then to extract the mouth Region of Interest (ROI). The mouth rectangle is rescaled to be 128×128 pixels, then it is transformed into a gray-scale format. Finally, the image-transformed-based features using the conventional DCT2 and the GVF are extracted from the mouth ROI of the subject. Only, the lowest-frequency 30-DCT or the first 30-GVF features were utilized in visual front-end.

To construct the AVSR pipeline, the extracted audio and visual feature vectors are linearly interpolated then fused together into a single audio-visual feature vector. Then, these features were fed to either the HMM-based or deep BRNN-based speech recognizer for classification, as shown in Figs. 3 and 4.

4.2 Audio-only Speech Recognition

Table 1 shows a comparison between the performance of the HMM_a and $BRNN_v$ ASR models after utilizing MFCC or GAF features in the audio front-ends. It shows that the use of $BRNN_a$ model outperformed the HMM_a model under clean and noisy conditions. Furthermore, the utilization of GAF leads to significant improvement of the system performance by 2.52% and 1.07% for HMM_a and $BRNN_a$ models, respectively, over the traditional MFCC features. This clearly confirms that GAF contain beneficial information that improves the ASR.

Table 1. Word Error Rate results of the HMM_a and $BRNN_a$ ASR models with MFCC or GAF as input features.

Model	Audio Feats.	Avg. WER [%]
HMM_a	MFCC	15
HMM_a	GAF	12.48
$BRNN_a$	MFCC	10.42
$BRNN_a$	**GAF**	**9.35**

Figure 5 demonstrates that the $BRNN_a$ model is more robust to noise than the HMM_a model. For example, the proposed deep ASR model consisting of GAF followed by BRNN, outperforms the conventional MFCC-HMM_a model by a large percentage difference by reducing the WER from 40% to 24.64% with about 38.4% relative improvement at -10 dB. In addition, a significant improvement was observed in the performance of both models when feeding them with GAF instead of MFCC features. For example, the use of GAF in both the HMM_a and the $BRNN_a$ models significantly improves system performance by reducing the WER from 40% to 33.11% with about 17.22% relative improvement, and from 27.78% to 24.64% with about 11.3% relative improvement, respectively, at −10 dB. The results demonstrate that the GAF-BRNN$_a$ model attained better results compared to the other three ASR models as it achieves the lowest WER. However, it is obvious that the performance of all ASR models would decrease dramatically if the SNR descends.

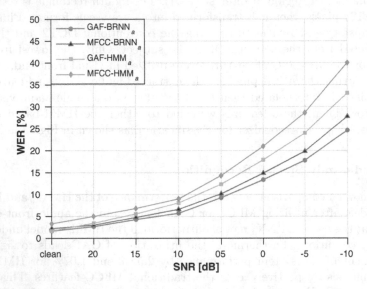

Fig. 5. Performance comparison between the HMM$_a$ and BRNN$_a$ ASR models using MFCC or GAF as input features at different SNR levels.

4.3   Visual-only Speech Recognition

Table 2 shows a comparison between the performance of the HMM$_v$ and BRNN$_v$ VSR models after utilizing DCT or GVF features in the visual front-ends. It demonstrates that the performance of the VSR system based on the BRNN$_v$ model is better than the HMM$_v$ model, especially when fed with GVF. The utilization of GVF in BRNN$_v$ model, termed as GVF-BRNN$_v$, significantly outperforms the traditional DCT-HMM$_v$ model by a very large percentage difference by reducing the WER from 46.15% to 20.16% with about 56.3% relative improvement. The results show that the deep GVF-BRNN$_v$ VSR model outperforms the other three VSR models.

4.4   Audio-Visual Speech Recognition

The AVSR experiments aim to demonstrate the usefulness of visual data and its significant impact in improving the system robustness, especially at low SNR levels. In these experiments, MFCC or GAF were used as audio features in addition to DCT or GVF, as visual features.

Table 2. Word Error Rate results of the HMM$_v$ and BRNN$_v$ VSR models with DCT or GVF as input features.

Model	Visual Feats.	Avg. WER [%]
HMM$_v$	DCT	46.15
HMM$_v$	GVF	38.36
BRNN$_v$	DCT	30.77
BRNN$_v$	**GVF**	**20.16**

Table 3. Word Error Rate results of the HMM$_{av}$ and BRNN$_{av}$ AVSR models with (MFCC and DCT) or (GAF and GVF) as input features.

Model	Audio Feats.	Visual Feats.	Avg. WER [%]
HMM$_{av}$	MFCC	DCT	12.09
HMM$_{av}$	GAF	GVF	10.89
BRNN$_{av}$	MFCC	DCT	10.21
BRNN$_{av}$	**GAF**	**GVF**	**7.82**

Table 3 compares the performance obtained after feeding the two EI AVSR models, the HMM$_{av}$ and BRNN$_{av}$ models, with a single feature vector of (MFCC and DCT) or (GAF and GVF) as input features. The results confirm that the proposed BRNN$_{av}$ model's performance is better than the HMM$_{av}$ model's performance. Moreover, the employment of (GAF and GVF) as input features in BRNN$_{av}$ attained a significant improvement in the AVSR system's performance, outperforming the conventional (MFCC and DCT)-HMM$_{av}$ model by a large percentage difference by reducing the WER from 12.09% to 7.82% with about 35.3% relative improvement.

Figure 6 shows a comparison between the best performance results of three different models; the BRNN$_a$, BRNN$_v$, and BRNN$_{av}$ models, at various SNR levels. The resulting graphs demonstrate that when the visual modality is integrated with audio modality to represent the speech recognition model, the performance is improved, particularly under noisy audio signal input. For example, the BRNN$_{av}$ AVSR model outperforms the BRNN$_a$ ASR model by a large margin by reducing the WER from 17.88% to 14.52% with 18.8% relative improvement under −10 dB SNR level.

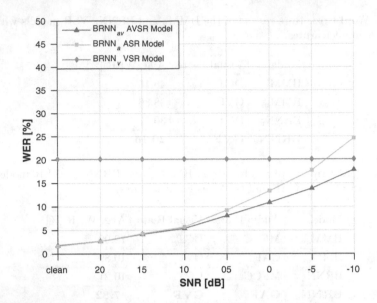

Fig. 6. Performance comparison of deep BRNN$_a$, BRNN$_v$, and BRNN$_{av}$ models using GAF as audio features and GVF as visual features at different SNR levels.

5   Conclusions

In this work, we presented a deep AVSR framework based on LSTM-BRNN network that incorporates the Gabor filters to generate a set of robust spectro-temporal audio and visual features. The experimental results demonstrate that the proposed framework attained superior performance on the CUAVE dataset when compared to the conventional GMM-HMM-based framework which uses the same audio and visual front-ends. In addition, the GAF and the GVF features achieved significant improvement in the performance of the continuous digit recognition problem compared with the traditional audio and visual features, especially in noisy environments. In the future work, we will extend our work to include an End-to-End deep AVSR model that utilizes the Gabor filters and evaluate its performance.

References

1. Chang, S.Y., Morgan, N.: Robust CNN-based speech recognition with Gabor filter kernels. In: Fifteenth Annual Conference of the International Speech Communication Association (2014)
2. Feng, W., Guan, N., Li, Y., Zhang, X., Luo, Z.: Audio visual speech recognition with multimodal recurrent neural networks. In: IEEE International Joint Conference on Neural Networks (IJCNN), pp. 681–688. IEEE (2017)
3. Gabor, D.: Theory of communication. Part 1: the analysis of information. J. Inst. Electr. Eng. Part III Radio Commun. Eng. **93**(26), 429–441 (1946)

4. Graves, A., Fernández, S., Gomez, F., Schmidhuber, J.: Connectionist temporal classification: labelling unsegmented sequence data with recurrent neural networks. In: Proceedings of the 23rd International Conference on Machine Learning, pp. 369–376. ACM (2006)
5. Graves, A., Jaitly, N.: Towards end-to-end speech recognition with recurrent neural networks. In: International Conference on Machine Learning, pp. 1764–1772 (2014)
6. Hannun, A., et al.: Deep speech: scaling up end-to-end speech recognition. arXiv:1412.5567 (2014)
7. Hochreiter, S., Schmidhuber, J.: Long short-term memory. Neural Comput. **9**(8), 1735–1780 (1997)
8. Luan, S., Chen, C., Zhang, B., Han, J., Liu, J.: Gabor convolutional networks. IEEE Trans. Image Process. **27**, 4357–4366 (2018)
9. McGurk, H., MacDonald, J.: Hearing lips and seeing voices. Nature **264**(5588), 746–748 (1976)
10. Mesgarani, N., David, S., Shamma, S.: Representation of phonemes in primary auditory cortex: how the brain analyzes speech. In: IEEE International Conference on Acoustics, Speech and Signal Processing (ICASSP), vol. 4, pp. 765–768. IEEE (2007)
11. Meshgini, S., Aghagolzadeh, A., Seyedarabi, H.: Face recognition using Gabor-based direct linear discriminant analysis and support vector machine. Comput. Electr. Eng. **39**(3), 727–745 (2013)
12. Nakamura, S.: Statistical multimodal integration for audio-visual speech processing. IEEE Trans. Neural Netw. **13**(4), 854–866 (2002)
13. Noda, K., Yamaguchi, Y., Nakadai, K., Okuno, H.G., Ogata, T.: Audio-visual speech recognition using deep learning. Appl. Intell. **42**(4), 722–737 (2015)
14. Patterson, E.K., Gurbuz, S., Tufekci, Z., Gowdy, J.N.: CUAVE: a new audio-visual database for multimodal human-computer interface research. In: Proceedings of IEEE International Conference on Acoustics, Speech, and Signal Processing (ICASSP), Orlando, Florida, USA, vol. 2, pp. II-2017–II-2020. IEEE (2002)
15. Petridis, S., Li, Z., Pantic, M.: End-to-end visual speech recognition with LSTMs. arXiv:1701.05847 (2017)
16. Petridis, S., Pantic, M.: Deep complementary bottleneck features for visual speech recognition. In: IEEE International Conference on Acoustics, Speech and Signal Processing (ICASSP), pp. 2304–2308. IEEE (2016)
17. Shen, L., Bai, L., Fairhurst, M.: Gabor wavelets and general discriminant analysis for face identification and verification. Image Vis. Comput. **25**(5), 553–563 (2007)
18. Thanda, A., Venkatesan, S.M.: Audio visual speech recognition using deep recurrent neural networks. In: Schwenker, F., Scherer, S. (eds.) MPRSS 2016. LNCS (LNAI), vol. 10183, pp. 98–109. Springer, Cham (2017). https://doi.org/10.1007/978-3-319-59259-6_9
19. Viola, P., Jones, M.J.: Robust real-time face detection. Int. J. Comput. Vis. **57**(2), 137–154 (2004)
20. Zhang, B., Gao, Y., Zhao, S., Liu, J.: Local derivative pattern versus local binary pattern: face recognition with high-order local pattern descriptor. IEEE Trans. Image Process. **19**(2), 533–544 (2010)

Evolutionary Algorithms for the Design of Neural Network Classifiers for the Classification of Pain Intensity

Danila Mamontov[1], Iana Polonskaia[1], Alina Skorokhod[1], Eugene Semenkin[1], Viktor Kessler[2], and Friedhelm Schwenker[2(✉)]

[1] Reshetnev Siberian State University of Science and Technology,
31 Krasnoyarskiy Rabochiy Prospect, Krasnoyarsk 660014, Russia
{mamontov.bs,yanapolonskaya1413,skorokhodav,eugenesemenkin}@yandex.ru
[2] Institute of Neural Information Processing, Ulm University,
James Franck Ring, 89081 Ulm, Germany
{viktor.kessler,friedhelm.schwenker}@uni-ulm.de

Abstract. In this paper we present a study on multi-modal pain intensity recognition based on video and bio-physiological sensor data. The newly recorded *SenseEmotion* dataset consisting of 40 individuals, each subjected to three gradually increasing levels of painful heat stimuli, has been used for the evaluation of the proposed algorithms. We propose and evaluated evolutionary algorithms for the design and adaptation of the structure of deep artificial neural network architectures. Feedforward Neural Network and Recurrent Neural Network have been considered for the optimisation by using a Self-Configuring Genetic Algorithm (Self-CGA) and Self-Configuring Genetic Programming (SelfCGP).

Keywords: Multimodal pain intensity recognition ·
Evolutionary algorithm · Neural network

1 Introduction

Automatic pain and emotion recognition have been developed based on a specific modality such as video signals, particularly facial expressions [7,15,21,22,30,32] or biophysiological signals [1,3,5,10,12,16,17]. More recently, multi-modal systems where several modalities are combined to improve the pain intensity recognition performance have been investigated [2,8,9,13,14,19,33]. In recent works also the audio modality has been successfully applied to pain intensity estimation [29,31], but still the most common modalities involved in the assessment of pain intensity are the video and biophysiological channels.

Nowadays, artificial Neural Networks (ANNs) are considered to be powerful methods for pattern recognition and for data analysis [23,24], in particular, the so-called deep neural networks have achieved enormous attention in recent times. However, the design of an ANN architecture for a classification or estimation

© Springer Nature Switzerland AG 2019
F. Schwenker and S. Scherer (Eds.): MPRSS 2018, LNAI 11377, pp. 84–100, 2019.
https://doi.org/10.1007/978-3-030-20984-1_8

task is still an open issue and the success of an ANN-architecture is typically highly depending on the experience of the machine learning or ANN engineer. Automatic generation, design and evaluation of ANN architectures would be a useful concept as in many problems the optimal architecture is not known beforehand. Typically, developers use a trial and error method to determine the ANN-structure.

Here is a brief list of hyper-parameters that people often vary by hand during ANN hyper optimisation: learning rate, batch size, training epoch, types of layers, number of layers, activation function for the neurons in different layers, and the dropout parameter. In our experimental study we are focussing mainly on the following hyper-parameters: number of layers and their types, number of neurons per layer and their activation functions.

In this paper, we propose to use Evolutionary Algorithms (EAs) for the ANN structure adaptation. We use two types of ANNs: Feedforward Neural Network (FNN) and Recurrent Neural Network (RNN). FNN and RNN structures are optimised using a Self-Configuring Genetic Algorithm (SelfCGA) and Self-Configuring Genetic Programming (SelfCGP) accordingly, borrowed from [25,26]. Self-Configuring modifications allow us to overcome the problems of selecting settings for the Genetic Algorithm (GA) and Genetic Programming (GP).

We use the Keras framework [4] in Python to train and build ANNs.

The remainder of this work is organised as follows. Section 2 consists of the description of the dataset. Section 3 has a short description of the Self-Configuring technique for EAs used for the ANN structure adaptation. In Sect. 6 a description of Particle Swarm Optimisation with parasitic behaviour (PSOPB) for feature selection is provided. Experiments as well as the corresponding results are presented in Sect. 7 followed by the discussion and conclusion in Sect. 8.

2   Dataset Description

The data utilized in the present work was recently collected with the goal of generating a multimodal corpus designed specifically for research in the domain of emotion and pain recognition. It consists of 40 participants (20 male, 20 female), each subjected to two sessions of experiments of about 40 min each, during which several pain and emotion stimuli were triggered and the demeanour of each participant was recorded using audio, video and biophysiological sensors.

The pain stimuli were elicited through heat generated by a Medoc Pathway thermal simulator[1]. The experiment was repeated for each participant twice, each time with the ATS thermode attached to a different forearm (left and right). Before the data was recorded, each participant's pain threshold temperature and pain tolerance temperature were determined. Based on both temperatures, an intermediate heat stimulation temperature was computed such that the range between both the threshold and tolerance temperatures was divided into 2 equally spaced ranges.

---

[1] http://medoc-web.com/products/pathway-model-ats/.

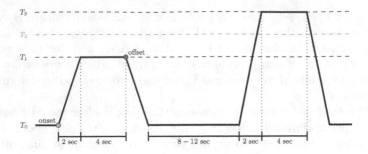

Fig. 1. Pain stimulation. T_0: baseline temperature (32 °C); T_1: pain threshold temperature; T_2: intermediate temperature; T_3: pain tolerance temperature.

A specific emotional elicitation was triggered simultaneously to each pain elicitation in the form of pictures and video clips. The latter were carefully selected with the purpose of triggering specific emotional responses. This allowed a categorisation of the emotion stimuli using a two-dimensional valence-arousal space in the following groups: positive (positive valence, high arousal); negative (negative valence, low arousal); neutral (neutral valence, neutral arousal).

Each heat temperature (pain stimulation) was triggered randomly 30 times with a randomised pause lasting between 8 and 12 s between consecutive stimuli. The randomised and simultaneous emotion stimuli were distributed for each heat temperature (pain stimulation) as well as the baseline temperature (no pain stimulation) as follows: 10 positive, 10 negative and 10 neutral emotion elicitations. Each stimulation consisted of a 2-s onset during which the temperature was gradually elevated starting from the baseline temperature until the specific heat temperature was reached. Following this, the attained temperature was maintained for 4 s before being gradually decreased until the baseline temperature was reached. A recovery phase of 8–12 s followed before the next pain stimulation was elicited (see Fig. 1 for more details).

Therefore, each participant is represented by two sets of data, each one representing the experiments conducted on each forearm (left and right). Each dataset consists of 120 pain stimuli with 30 stimuli per temperature (T_0: baseline, T_1: threshold, T_2: intermediate, T_3: tolerance), and 120 emotion stimuli with 40 stimuli per emotion category (positive, negative, neutral).

The synchronous data recorded from the experiments consists of 3 high-resolution video streams from 3 different perspectives, 2 audio lines recorded respectively from a headset and a directional microphone, and 4 physiological channels, namely the electromyographic activity of the trapezius muscle (EMG), the galvanic skin response (GSR), the electrocardiogram (ECG) and the respiration (RSP). Furthermore, an additional video and audio stream were recorded using the Microsoft Kinect sensor.

The focus of the present work is the investigation of the relevance of both audio and video channels regarding the task of pain intensity recognition. Thus the recognition of the different categories of emotion or the impact of the emotion stimuli on pain recognition will not be investigated.

In this paper, we have been concentrated on a binary classification of pain level according to T_0 and T_3 temperature. All approaches have been tested on two parts of the dataset for the left and right forearms.

3 Evolutionary Algorithms

Evolutionary algorithms (EAs) are common population-based methods used for global optimisation problems [6]. During this investigation, we take into account two EAs: the Genetic Algorithm, which represents solutions in a binary string form, and the Genetic Programming algorithm, where solutions are encoded as binary trees. The main advantage of EAs in contradistinction to gradient methods lies in their "creativity" - due to the recombination pieces of solutions from the population, unexpectedly effective results can arise that would otherwise be difficult to predict. However, at the same time, the main disadvantage is the large amount of computation required for this in the case of poorly selected settings. Indeed, in the course of evolution, it is necessary to test many bad hypotheses. To address this problem, it is necessary to use modified algorithms. For instance, effective combinations of evolutionary operators allow an optimal solution to be found with fewer objective function evaluations.

3.1 Self-configuration of EAs

Both GA and GP have many adjustable parameters. Since the number of parameter combinations is large, the use of brute force is not always possible. In order to overcome this defect in the study, we use the operator-based Self-Configuration technique. The main idea is that this technique should choose the most useful combinations of operators from all available ones in GA and GP. In the beginning, all operators have the same probability to be chosen for new offspring generation. During the course of work, Self-Configuration changes these probabilities based on the offspring fitness improvement generated by the a certain operator. There are several evolutionary operators, namely selection, crossover and level of mutation.

We have added the following types of operators for the Self-Configuration in this study. There are three types of selection: proportional, rank-based and tournament with three tournament sizes (2, 5 and 9). Three types of crossover (one-point, two-point, and uniform) for GA and two types (standard and one-point) for GP are included. Three levels of mutation: weak $\frac{1}{5*n}$, medium $\frac{1}{n}$, and strong $\frac{5}{n}$ are also included. Where n is an actual depth of a tree in GP and a length of a binary string in GA.

The general procedure of SelfCGA and SelfCGP:

1. Set equal probabilities for all possible options of each operator type (each of the operators has its own probability distribution)
2. Initialize the first population
3. Select types of selection, recombination and mutation
4. Identify parents using the selected selection operator
5. Cross parents using the selected crossover type
6. Mutate the offspring with the selected probability level of mutation
7. Estimate the fitness of the new offspring
8. Repeat steps 3–7 until the new generation is formed
9. Recalculate the operator type probabilities using the average fitness of offspring obtained with the certain operator
10. Check the stop conditions, and if it is not reached, go to step 3, otherwise stop the search and take the offspring with the best fitness as a final solution.

3.2   Fitness Function

The fitness function is an indicator of the solution success in EAs. It ranges from 0 to 1 (a perfect solution would have a fitness of 1). We should define this function for each certain problem we solve. In this research, we should evaluate the effectiveness of different ANN structures. Usually, in the course of ANN training, cross-entropy is used as a loss function for backpropagation. The cross-entropy ranges between 0 and 1 (a perfect model would have a cross-entropy loss of 0). It allows ANN to be trained most effectively. Therefore, we take the cross-entropy (in the case of binary classification problems it is the binary version) for calculating the fitness function as follows:

$$fitness = \frac{1}{1 + mean\_loss} \qquad (1)$$

Where $mean\_loss$ is the average loss of participant independent leave one participant out cross validation performance with m participants from the dataset:

$$mean\_loss = \frac{\sum_{i=1}^{m} binary\_crossentropy_i}{m} \qquad (2)$$

m is equal to 5 within the frame of SelfCGP and SelfCGA work. After the final structures are found, they are tested on the whole dataset with m equals 40.

4   RNN Structure Optimisation Using SelfCGP

As is mentioned above, we apply SelfCGP for the RNN structure adaptation. SelfCGP is already successfully used in the design of FNNs for solving various data analysis problems [27].

Keras has several kinds of recurrent layers. The following layer types have been used: Simple recurrent neural network (a fully-connected RNN where the output is to be fed back to input); LSTM (a long-short term memory RNN); Dense (a regular densely-connected NN layer). In addition, we take Dropout layers (randomly setting a fraction rate of input units to 0 at each update during the training time, which helps prevent overfitting) [28]. It is very important to give an opportunity for SelfCGP to design RNNs with Dropout layers. It is worth noting that ANNs cannot consist only of Dropout layers, so we include them in the functional set, but not in the terminal one. Next, we need to define several different coefficients of Dropout, for instance, $0.1, 0.2, \ldots, 0.9$.

4.1 Terminal and Functional Sets

The terminal set can contain a lot of variations of layers with the different parameters described above. In this study, we have included follow layer types in the terminal set: SimpleRNN, LSTM, GRU, and Dense layers. In addition, all the activation functions available in Keras have been included in the terminal set: softmax, elu, selu, softplus, softsign, relu, tanh, sigmoid, hard_sigmoid and linear. The range of the available number of neurons per layer has been set from 1 to 40.

Therefore, the terminal set contains 400 elements (all possible combinations of layers, activation functions and numbers of neurons).

The functional set should include possible operations on elements from the terminal set. We have defined two operations to be included in the functional set:

1. Sequential union ("+")
2. Sequential union with additional Dropout layer ("+" Dropout with coefficients $\{0.1, 0.2, \ldots, 0.9\}$).

4.2 The Structure Encoding Description

GP uses binary trees for encoding all structures (unlike GA that uses binary strings). In this study, we propose using the following method of encoding ANN structures into trees. For instance, Fig. 2 shows the structure encoded into the tree.

The code below represents the decoded structure from Fig. 2 already in a form suitable for Keras. All leaves belong to the terminal set, and at the same time, nodes with two child belong to the functional set.

```
model = Sequential()
# Encoded part starts
model.add(Dense(32, activation='tanh'))
model.add(Dropout(0.5))
model.add(LSTM(64,return_sequences=True ))
model.add(Dropout(0.3))
model.add(SimpleRNN(16,return_sequences=True ))
model.add(Dense(18, activation='relu'))
model.add(LSTM(28))
model.add(Dense(y.shape[1], activation='softmax'))
# Encoded part ends
```

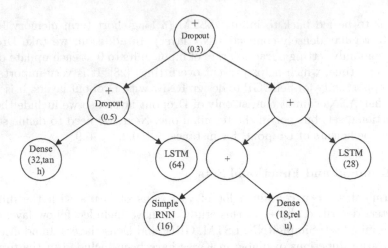

Fig. 2. The example of encoding the neural network structure into the tree for GP

This kind of encoding allows to encode various types of ANN structures with an unlimited number of layers. We prevent the design of trees with only Dense layers by using a restriction on the presence of at least one recurrent layer.

4.3   Experiment Description

As a baseline, we take FNN with one hidden layer and 40 neurons calculated by the following function:

$$N_{neurons} = \frac{n_{inputs} + n_{outputs}}{2} + 1 \tag{3}$$

When using GSR features $n_{inputs} = 77$ and $n_{outputs} = 2$ then $N_{neurons} = 40$.

The final best structure found by SelfCGP is tested on all 40 patients using the cross-validation described above. After that, we calculate the Student's t-test to determine statistically significant differences among all results.

The problem we solve has no time dependence, and at first glance, it would appear that the use of RNNs will be ineffective. However, according to [11], RNNs can surpass the effectiveness of FNNs for problems with no time dependency. Since an RNN requires the presence of a time factor for learning, but the problem is static, in this paper we duplicate the input feature vector in time. Thus, a constant signal is emitted. We have defined the input vector repeats for 3 and 5 times ($SelfCGP_{3st}$ and $SelfCGP_{5st}$) for tests. We also compare training on 1 and 3 epochs. The main parameters of SelfCGP are: the population size is 100 individuals, the number of generations is 100, the maximum depth is 3, and the fully growth at initialization step.

5 FNN Structure Optimisation Using SelfCGA

We have tested two different methods of FNN encoding. The first one uses only Dense layers, but the second one uses Dense and Dropout layers. In this case, SelfCGA is used for finding the optimal number of neurons, layer activation function and the total number of layers. The length that describes one part of the FNN (Dense layer + Dropout layer) is divided into four sets. The first set represents the type of activation function of the Dense layer. The second represents the number of neurons in the Dense layer. The third set represents the presence or absence of the Dropout layer after Dense, and then the fourth set represents the fraction of the input units to drop. The FNN in the genotype can be represented as shown in Figs. 3 and 4. After the second and fourth layers of the dense type, the layers of the droplet types do not follow, and the next part of the network immediately begins. The architecture of each network is coded into the chromosomes of SelfCGA, where each chromosome is composed of $(n - m) * 4$ genes. n is the maximal number of layers (or we can call it parts of the network: Dense + Dropout), which must be selected before running the program, m is the number of inactive layers (parts of the neural network which contain 0 neurons on the Dense layer not expressed in the phenotype). If we use only one type of layer, we can remove the part which describes Dense layer, and if we use more types of layers, we can add more parts in the string.

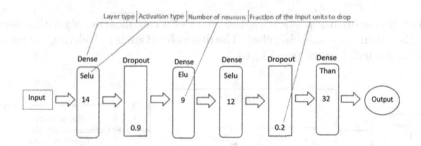

Fig. 3. Example of the NN architecture

FNN is optimised by the Adam algorithm.

6 Feature Selection Using PSOPB

Within this research, the dimension of the feature space is reduced by Particle Swarm Optimisation with parasitic behavior (PSOPB) [20]. This dataset contains big data (data of large dimensions). Thus, the solution of the classification problem becomes a complicated task for some algorithms. For example, using an artificial neural network, the number of neurons in the first layer is equal to the dimensionality of the feature space, and the number of weights that any

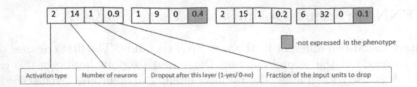

Fig. 4. Example of a genotype. The genotype defines the NN architecture from Fig. 3. In this case, second and forth Dropout layers are an inactive.

training algorithm needs to find could be even greater. Thus, the problem of consuming a large number of resources, both temporary and memory, arises. A possible solution is to reduce the feature space. The decrease dimension of the feature space has already been made by classical methods, such as PCA, so another approach was chosen to solve this problem. Each attribute is evaluated by a certain feature. Thus, the string of input classification parameters is the vector of binomial values for the optimisation algorithm (see Fig. 5) [18].

Features	x_1	x_2	...	x_n
«Particle» of PSOPB	1	0	...	1

Fig. 5. Example of converting an attributes vector into a "particle" vector

The fitness of the "particle" is the result of a classification algorithm (accuracy, f1-measure or something else). The fitness function is a "deleting" of parameters with a null feature (see Fig. 6).

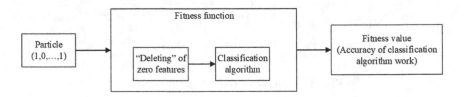

Fig. 6. Example of Fitness values calculation

RNN is chosen like the Fitness function of PSOPB.

The structure of RNN contains one hidden layer with 40 neurons of the LSTM type, n input neurons (depends on the number of features) and two output neurons.

```
model.add(RepeatVector(3, input_shape=(len(train_data.loc[0]),)))
model.add(LSTM(40))
model.add(Dense(traint_labels.shape[1], activation='softmax'))
```

Accuracy is chosen like the fitness value of the particle.

7   Experiments

7.1   Feature Selection Results

Experiments are conducted using GSR features. It has two parts: right and left, so the results of the PSOPB working are two binomial vectors of parameter coefficients.

PSOPB with 10 generations and 30 individuals in the population found two binomial vectors for each ("left" and "right" forearms) problem. The strings below are the final results of PSOPB. These strings show which GSR feature takes part in the designing of the classifier and which does not.

For the left forearm:

$$X = [0, 0, 1, 1, 1, 0, 1, 0, 0, 0, 0, 0, 0, 1, 0, 0, 0, 0, 1, 0, 1, 0, 0, 1, 0, 1,$$
$$1, 1, 1, 0, 1, 1, 1, 0, 1, 0, 0, 0, 0, 1, 1, 1, 1, 1, 0, 0, 1, 1, 1, 1, 0, 1,$$
$$1, 1, 0, 0, 1, 1, 0, 1, 0, 1, 1, 1, 1, 1, 1, 0, 1, 1, 1, 0, 1, 1, 1, 0, 1]$$

For the right forearm:

$$X = [0, 1, 0, 0, 0, 1, 1, 0, 0, 0, 0, 1, 1, 1, 1, 0, 1, 0, 1, 1, 0, 0, 1, 1, 0,$$
$$1, 0, 1, 0, 1, 0, 0, 0, 1, 1, 1, 0, 0, 0, 1, 1, 0, 0, 0, 1, 1, 1, 1, 0, 0,$$
$$0, 0, 1, 0, 1, 1, 1, 0, 0, 1, 1, 1, 0, 0, 0, 1, 1, 0, 0, 1, 1, 1, 1, 0, 1, 1, 0]$$

Therefore, we have 44 active features for the "left" part and 39 active features for the "right" part.

The results of the work of the two algorithms are compared with each other by the Student's t-test. Experiments are conducted in different conditions to find the relation between RNN structure or settings and the work of PSOPB (Table 1). The mean accuracy was obtained by conducting 40 runs with different patients for testing. 39 people are taken for training on the RNN and one person for the test.

7.2   RNN Optimisation Results

The following structures are found by SelfCGP. For the left forearm problem:

```
1st layer - GRU with 29 neurons and activation='linear'
2nd layer - SimpleRNN with 37 neurons and activation='linear'
3rd layer - GRU with 26 neurons and activation='softsign'
4th layer - SimpleRNN with 37 neurons and activation='linear'
```

As we can see, there are 4 layers with only GRU and SimpleRNN types of layers.

For the right forearm problem:

```
1st layer - SimpleRNN with 30 neurons and activation=' tanh '
2nd layer - SimpleRNN with 40 neurons and activation=' tanh '
3rd layer - SimpleRNN with 40 neurons and activation=' tanh '
```

Table 1. RNN accuracy on original data (77 features) and reduced by PSOPB (44 for Left Forearm and 39 for Right Forearm)

Forearm	Batch size	Epochs	Number of features	Mean accuracy, %	Std, %	p-value
Left	32	1	44	79.42	12.24	0.94
			77	79.21	11.81	
		3	44	80.95	12.37	0.81
			77	81.62	12.24	
	64	1	44	78.44	12.03	0.8
			77	77.77	11.49	
		3	44	79.93	12.22	1
			77	79.93	12.22	
Right	32	1	39	78.67	13.06	0.81
			77	79.40	12.87	
		3	39	80.15	13.27	0.95
			77	80.33	12.95	
	64	1	39	77.49	13.69	0.76
			77	78.43	12.75	
		3	39	79.52	13.45	0.92
			77	79.23	13.25	

In this case, there are only 3 SimpleRNN layers and "tanh" as an activation function for each layer.

The Table 2 shows the average participant independent leave one participant out cross validation performance.

As can be seen from the Table 2, the best average value for the classification accuracy is achieved by training in 3 epochs on the structure obtained with the help of SelfCGP and 3 time steps for the left forearm problem and 5 time steps for the right forearm problem (bold values). There are no statistically significant differences among all the results according to the Student's t-test.

PSOPB reduced the dimensionality from 77 to 44 for the left forearm problem. The best structure found by SelfCGP is:

```
1st layer - SimpleRNN with 40 neurons and activation = 'tanh'
2nd layer - Dropout (0.2)
3rd layer - SimpleRNN with 40 neurons and activation = 'tanh'
4th layer - Dropout (0.1)
5rd layer - SimpleRNN with 40 neurons and activation = 'tanh'
6rd layer - SimpleRNN with 40 neurons and activation = 'tanh'
```

Table 2. SelfCGP without reduction

	Left forearm			Right forearm		
	Baseline	$SelfCGP_{3st}$	$SelfCGP_{5st}$	Baseline	$SelfCGP_{3st}$	$SelfCGP_{5st}$
1 epoch						
Mean accuracy, %	77.17	79.92	79.58	77.87	79.07	78.82
Std, %	11.94	11.78	12.54	12.18	13.44	12.58
Min, %	47.45	50.84	52.54	44.99	49.15	49.15
Max, %	96.61	100	100	96.66	100.0	98.30
3 epochs						
Mean accuracy, %	81.24	**81.54**	81.37	79.31	80.68	**80.85**
Std, %	11.73	12.61	12.64	14.02	12.45	11.93
Min, %	52.54	50.84	53.44	44.99	52.54	51.72
Max, %	100.0	100	100	98.30	100.0	100.0

For the right forearm problem PSOPB allowed the dimensionality to be reduced from 77 to 39. SelfCGP found the following structure:

```
1st layer - SimpleRNN with 28 neurons and activation = 'tanh'
2nd layer - Dropout (0.1)
3rd layer - SimpleRNN with 32 neurons and activation = 'linear '
4th layer - GRU with 40 neurons and activation = 'linear'
```

The Table 3 shows the average for the RNN with reduced dimension dataset participant independent leave one participant out cross validation performance.

Table 3. SelfCGP with reduction

	Left forearm			Right forearm		
	Baseline	$SelfCGP_{3st}$	$SelfCGP_{5st}$	Baseline	$SelfCGP_{3st}$	$SelfCGP_{5st}$
1 epoch						
Mean accuracy, %	77.17	79.24	78.63	77.87	78.90	78.55
Std, %	11.94	11.24	12.95	12.18	14.08	13.79
Min, %	47.45	55.93	49.15	44.99	41.66	41.66
Max, %	96.61	96.61	98.33	96.66	98.30	98.30
3 epochs						
Mean accuracy, %	**81.24**	80.61	79.88	79.31	79.73	**79.94**
Std, %	11.73	12.74	12.64	14.02	13.67	13.41
Min, %	52.54	50.84	54.99	44.99	46.66	46.66
Max, %	100.0	98.33	98.33	98.30	98.33	100.0

Here there are also no statistically significant differences among all the results according to the Student's t-test.

7.3   FNN Optimisation Results

Below are two example Neural Network topologies found by SelfCGA that showed the best results.

The structure found by the SelfCGA for the group of features of GSR on the data of the right forearm is given:

```
1st layer - Dense with 23 neurons and activation function='elu'
2nd layer - Dense with 29 neurons and activation function='tanh'
3rd layer - Dense with 13 neurons and activation function='selu'
```

The structure was found using the self-configuring GA for group video features using the data of the left forearm:

```
1st layer - Dense with 9 neurons and activation function='linear'
2nd layer - Dropout (0.281250)
3rd layer - Dense with 16 neurons and activation function='linear'
4th layer - Dropout (0.210938)
5th layer - Dense with 16 neurons and activation function='linear'
6th layer - Dropout (0.398438)
7th layer - Dense with 11 neurons and activation function='linear'
8th layer - Dropout (0.078125)
9th layer - Dense with 8 neurons and activation function='sigmoid'
10th layer - Dropout (0.296875)
11th layer - Dense with 18 neurons and activation function='softsign'
12th layer - Dense with 9 neurons and activation function='selu'
13th layer - Dense with 2 neurons and activation function=' softsign'
14th layer - Dense with 17 neurons and activation function='tanh'
15th layer - Dense with 16 neurons and activation function=' softsign'
```

These architectures outperforms the other found models. Still, its performance is not significantly better.

Tables 4 and 5 show the results of mean accuracy for different neural network architectures obtained by cross-validation. The Table 4 includes the results which was get using GSR features, and the Table 5 includes results for video features. 1st encoding type means that SelfCGA used only dense layers in neural network arcitecture construction process, and 2st encoding type means that SelfCGA could build neural networks using Dense and Dropout layers.

Table 4. SelfCGA for GSR features

Forearm	№ of architecture	The mean accuracy and the std, %	
		1st encoding type	2nd encoding type
Left	1	81.5 (±1.8)	81.6 (±2)
	2	81.5 (±1.8)	80.3 (±2)
	3	80.8 (±1.9)	-
Right	1	82.1 (±2.1)	82.29 (±2.1)
	2	81.2 (±2.3)	82.1 (±2.1)
	3	81.6 (±2.1)	81.79 (±2)

Table 5. SelfCGA for video features

Forearm	№ of architecture	The mean accuracy and the std, %	
		1st encoding type	2nd encoding type
Left	1	63.6 (±2)	65.4 (±2.1)
	2	65.2 (±2.3)	64.7 (±2.1)
Right	1	64.4 (±2)	64.2 (±2)
	2	63.9 (±2)	65.6 (⊥1.8)

8   Conclusion

In this paper, we have presented two EAs for the design of ANN classifiers. With the obtained results, we can state that SelfCGP allows the structure of RNNs to be optimised, but the results of the Student's t-test do not allow us to assert that the obtained improvements are statistically significant for these problems. Reducing the dimension space by PSOPB did not change the accuracy in the work of the FNN in statistical terms, but the dimension space was reduced by about half. It is better to calculate big and complicate models like an RNN with an optimised structure by SelfCGA or SelfCGP on this dataset. Therefore, we can conclude that this method of reducing the dimension space can be implemented in work with the SenseEmotion dataset.

Acknowledgements. The reported study was funded by Krasnoyarsk Regional Fund of Science according to the participation in the internship *Recurrent neural Networks, Deep Learning for Video retrieval*. We gratefully acknowledge the support of NVIDIA Corporation with the donation of the Tesla K40 GPU used for this research. The work of FS was support by the *SenseEmotion* project funded by the Federal Ministry of Education and Research (BMBF).

References

1. Amirian, M., Kächele, M., Schwenker, F.: Using radial basis function neural networks for continuous and discrete pain estimation from bio-physiological signals. In: Schwenker, F., Abbas, H.M., El Gayar, N., Trentin, E. (eds.) ANNPR 2016. LNCS (LNAI), vol. 9896, pp. 269–284. Springer, Cham (2016). https://doi.org/10.1007/978-3-319-46182-3_23
2. Aung, M.S.H., et al.: The automatic detection of chronic pain-related expression: requirements, challenges and multimodal dataset. IEEE Trans. Affect. Comput. **7**, 435–451 (2016)
3. Bellmann, P., Thiam, P., Schwenker, F.: Multi-classifier-systems: architectures, algorithms and applications. In: Pedrycz, W., Chen, S.-M. (eds.) Computational Intelligence for Pattern Recognition. SCI, vol. 777, pp. 83–113. Springer, Cham (2018). https://doi.org/10.1007/978-3-319-89629-8_4
4. Chollet, F., et al.: Keras (2015). https://keras.io
5. Chu, Y., Zhao, X., Yao, J., Zhao, Y., Wu, Z.: Physiological signals based quantitative evaluation method of the pain. In: Proceedings of the 19th IFAC World Congress, pp. 2981–2986 (2014)
6. Coello, C.A.C., Lamont, G.B., Van Veldhuizen, D.A., et al.: Evolutionary Algorithms for Solving Multi-objective Problems, vol. 5. Springer, New York (2007). https://doi.org/10.1007/978-0-387-36797-2
7. Florea, C., Florea, L., Vertan, C.: Learning pain from emotion: transferred hot data representation for pain intensity estimation. In: Agapito, L., Bronstein, M.M., Rother, C. (eds.) ECCV 2014. LNCS, vol. 8927, pp. 778–790. Springer, Cham (2015). https://doi.org/10.1007/978-3-319-16199-0_54
8. Glodek, M., Scherer, S., Schwenker, F.: Conditioned hidden Markov model fusion for multimodal classification. In: Twelfth Annual Conference of the International Speech Communication Association (2011)
9. Glodek, M., et al.: Multiple classifier systems for the classification of audio-visual emotional states. In: D'Mello, S., Graesser, A., Schuller, B., Martin, J.-C. (eds.) ACII 2011. LNCS, vol. 6975, pp. 359–368. Springer, Heidelberg (2011). https://doi.org/10.1007/978-3-642-24571-8_47
10. Gruss, S., et al.: Pain intensity recognition rates via biopotential feature patterns with support vector machines. PLoS ONE **10**, e0140330 (2015)
11. Hagenbuchner, M., Tsoi, A.C., Scarselli, F., Zhang, S.J.: A fully recursive perceptron network architecture. In: 2017 IEEE Symposium Series on Computational Intelligence (SSCI), pp. 1–8. IEEE (2017)
12. Kächele, M., Thiam, P., Amirian, M., Schwenker, F., Palm, G.: Methods for person-centered continuous pain intensity assessment from bio-physiological channels. IEEE J. Sel. Top. Signal Process. **10**, 854–864 (2016)
13. Kächele, M., et al.: Multimodal data fusion for person-independent, continuous estimation of pain intensity. In: Iliadis, L., Jayne, C. (eds.) EANN 2015. CCIS, vol. 517, pp. 275–285. Springer, Cham (2015). https://doi.org/10.1007/978-3-319-23983-5_26
14. Kächele, M., Werner, P., Al-Hamadi, A., Palm, G., Walter, S., Schwenker, F.: Biovisual fusion for person-independent recognition of pain intensity. In: Schwenker, F., Roli, F., Kittler, J. (eds.) MCS 2015. LNCS, vol. 9132, pp. 220–230. Springer, Cham (2015). https://doi.org/10.1007/978-3-319-20248-8_19

15. Kaltwang, S., Rudovic, O., Pantic, M.: Continuous pain intensity estimation from facial expressions. In: Bebis, G., et al. (eds.) ISVC 2012. LNCS, vol. 7432, pp. 368–377. Springer, Heidelberg (2012). https://doi.org/10.1007/978-3-642-33191-6_36

16. Kessler, V., Thiam, P., Amirian, M., Schwenker, F.: Pain recognition with camera photoplethysmography. In: 2017 Seventh International Conference on Image Processing Theory, Tools and Applications (IPTA), pp. 1–5. IEEE (2017)

17. Kestler, H., et al.: De-noising of high-resolution ECG signals by combining the discrete wavelet transform with the wiener filter. In: Computers in Cardiology, pp. 233–236. IEEE (1998)

18. Meshheryakov, R., Khodashinskij, I., Gusakova, E.: Evaluation of feature space for intrusion detection system. News of Southern Federal University. Tech. Sci. **12**(149) (2013)

19. Olugbade, T.A., Bianchi-Berthouze, N., Marquardt, N., Williams, A.C.: Pain level recognition using kinematics and muscle activity for physical rehabilitation in chronic pain. In: IEEE Proceedings of International Conference on Affective Computing and Intelligent Interaction, pp. 243–249 (2015)

20. Qin, Q., Cheng, S., Zhang, Q., Li, L., Shi, Y.: Biomimicry of parasitic behavior in a coevolutionary particle swarm optimization algorithm for global optimization. Appl. Soft Comput. **32**, 224–240 (2015)

21. Schels, M., Schwenker, F.: A multiple classifier system approach for facial expressions in image sequences utilizing GMM supervectors. In: 2010 20th International Conference on Pattern Recognition (ICPR), pp. 4251–4254. IEEE (2010)

22. Schmidt, M., Schels, M., Schwenker, F.: A hidden Markov model based approach for facial expression recognition in image sequences. In: Schwenker, F., El Gayar, N. (eds.) ANNPR 2010. LNCS (LNAI), vol. 5998, pp. 149–160. Springer, Heidelberg (2010). https://doi.org/10.1007/978-3-642-12159-3_14

23. Schwenker, F., Kestler, H.A., Palm, G.: Three learning phases for radial-basis-function networks. Neural Netw. **14**(4–5), 439–458 (2001)

24. Schwenker, F., Trentin, E.: Pattern classification and clustering: a review of partially supervised learning approaches. Pattern Recognit. Lett. **37**, 4–14 (2014)

25. Semenkin, E., Semenkina, M.: Self-configuring genetic algorithm with modified uniform crossover operator. In: Tan, Y., Shi, Y., Ji, Z. (eds.) ICSI 2012. LNCS, vol. 7331, pp. 414–421. Springer, Heidelberg (2012). https://doi.org/10.1007/978-3-642-30976-2_50

26. Semenkin, E., Semenkina, M.: Self-configuring genetic programming algorithm with modified uniform crossover. In: 2012 IEEE Congress on Evolutionary Computation (CEC), pp. 1–6. IEEE (2012)

27. Semenkin, E., Semenkina, M., Panfilov, I.: Neural network ensembles design with self-configuring genetic programming algorithm for solving computer security problems. In: Herrero, Á., et al. (eds.) International Joint Conference CISIS 2012-ICEUTE 2012-SOCO 2012 Special Sessions. AISC, vol. 189, pp. 25–32. Springer, Heidelberg (2013). https://doi.org/10.1007/978-3-642-33018-6_3

28. Srivastava, N., Hinton, G., Krizhevsky, A., Sutskever, I., Salakhutdinov, R.: Dropout: a simple way to prevent neural networks from overfitting. J. Mach. Learn. Res. **15**(1), 1929–1958 (2014)

29. Thiam, P., et al.: Multi-modal pain intensity recognition based on the sense emotion database. IEEE (2019)

30. Thiam, P., Kessler, V., Schwenker, F.: Hierarchical combination of video features for personalised pain level recognition. In: 25th European Symposium on Artificial Neural Networks, Computational Intelligence and Machine Learning, pp. 465–470 (2017)
31. Thiam, P., Schwenker, F.: Multi-modal data fusion for pain intensity assessment and classification. In: 2017 Seventh International Conference on Image Processing Theory, Tools and Applications (IPTA), pp. 1–6. IEEE (2017)
32. Werner, P., Al-Hamadi, A., Niese, R., Walter, S., Gruss, S., Traue, H.C.: Towards pain monitoring: facial expression, head pose, a new database, an automatic system and remaining challenges. In: Proceedings of the British Machine Vision Conference, pp. 1–13 (2013)
33. Werner, P., Al-Hamadi, A., Niese, R., Walter, S., Gruss, S., Traue, H.C.: Automatic pain recognition from video and biomedical signals. In: Proceedings of the International Conference on Pattern Recognition (ICPR), pp. 4582–4587 (2014)

Visualizing Facial Expression Features of Pain and Emotion Data

Jan Sellner, Patrick Thiam, and Friedhelm Schwenker[✉]

Institute of Neural Information Processing, Ulm University,
James Franck Ring, 89081 Ulm, Germany
{jan.sellner,patrick.thiam,friedhelm.schwenker}@uni-ulm.de

Abstract. Pain and emotions reveal important information about the state of a person and are often expressed via the face. Most of the time, systems which analyse these states consider only one type of expression. For pain, the medical context is a common scenario for automatic monitoring systems and it is not unlikely that emotions occur there as well. Hence, these systems should not confuse both types of expressions. To facilitate advances in this field, we use video data from the BioVid Heat Pain Database, extract *Action Unit (AU)* intensity features and conduct first analyses by creating several feature visualizations. We show that the AU usage pattern is more distinct for the pain, amusement and disgust classes than for the sadness, fear and anger classes. For the former, we present additional visualizations which reveal a clearer picture of the typically used AUs per expression by highlighting dependencies between AUs (joint usages). Finally, we show that the feature discrimination quality varies heavily across the 64 tested subjects.

Keywords: Pain · Emotions · Facial expression ·
Feature visualization · FACS · Action Unit

1 Introduction

Pain and emotions play both an important role in the life of a human being. The ability to signal these inner states is crucial for communication and they are often expressed non-verbally via facial expressions [6,8]. The automatic analysis of the face is beneficial in a variety of different scenarios and some applications have already been developed [2,5,21,25,26].

The usual motivation for pain recognition systems is the medical context [22,29] where systems should help patients which cannot express their state otherwise or when self-report is not available [10]. However, emotions are not necessarily absent in this context so that corresponding expressions may be shown as well [4]. Therefore, an automatic recognition system should be capable to distinguish both types of expressions.

It is also possible that emotions are experienced and displayed during painful phases [4]. For example, Hale et al. reported that patients which undergo routine blood tests also experience the emotions disgust, anger and fear [11].

© Springer Nature Switzerland AG 2019
F. Schwenker and S. Scherer (Eds.): MPRSS 2018, LNAI 11377, pp. 101–115, 2019.
https://doi.org/10.1007/978-3-030-20984-1_9

When patients show an increased number of affective states, it may even be an indication of the pain intensity [14].

In both cases, emotions and pain which co-occur and emotional expressions which accompany pain, it is important to detect the different kind of expressions reliably. To implement a detection system, data and extracted features are required. For the latter, it is helpful to first get a basic understanding of the features to see how they behave across classes.

Here, we are using data from the BioVid Heat Pain Database, describe the facial expressions in terms of *Action Unit (AU)* intensities and apply a qualitative analysis by showing some visualizations to better understand typical painful and emotional expressions. We are going to demonstrate how AUs are used across classes, illustrate the dependencies between the AUs and highlight subject-dependent differences. Knowledge from these visualizations can help to understand the result of a classifier system better.

The rest of this article is structured as follows: Sect. 2 reviews the current literature, Sect. 3 introduces the database and explains how we extract the features, three different visualizations are shown in Sects. 4 and 5 we discuss the results and give an outlook for future work.

2   Related Work

Pain has received a lot of attention in the facial expression recognition community and the tasks vary from the detection of pain, intensity estimation [23, 24] or the classification of faked versus real pain. An overview of these approaches can be found in [28]. The situation for emotions is similar as here also many approaches have been developed, e.g. to distinguish between a basic set of discrete emotions [18, 20, 31].

When considering both types of expressions, however, the number of contributions is less extensive. Simon et al. used short videos showing expressions from actors and successfully let subjects rate the clips [19]. In [16], Niese et al. used geometric 3D models to calculate facial distances based on facial landmarks and a Support Vector Machine to detect pain while considering four discrete emotions (joy surprise, anger and disgust) and the neutral class at the same time. Hammal et al. used videos of spontaneous expressions, a dynamic fusion process to include context information and tracked characteristic points throughout the video sequence to detect pain by also adding emotions to the training data [12].

For the BioVid database we are using here (see Sect. 3.1), there is currently no other work listed concerning both, pain and emotions [1].

3   Database and Features

3.1   Database

In the BioVid Heat Pain Database, experiments were conducted to collect data about pain and emotions. Several parameters were measured including facial expressions via video signals. The database consists of several parts and here we are using part A (neutral and pain videos) [27,29] and part E (emotion videos) [33].

Part A contains short-time videos of 5.5 s length (138 frames) for 64 subjects (subject identifiers can be found in Fig. 6) and 20 videos per class (neutral and pain). The data was collected in an experiment were heat pain in different levels was induced to subjects. Here, we select only videos corresponding to the highest pain level and choose subjects who also participated in part E and who showed sufficient facial expressiveness [30].

In part E, five discrete emotions (amusement, sadness, anger, disgust and fear) were elicited via film clips. A frontal video was captured for each subject while he or she was watching three clips. The subject rated each clip and the video corresponding to the highest rating was kept. Additionally, the subject rated the clips according to the experienced emotional level (for each of the five emotions as well as valence and arousal). The subject videos are of different length (ranging from 27 to 241 s) and there is only one video per subject and emotion available.

In total, this results in seven classes, 64 subjects and 45 videos per subject.

3.2 Facial Expressions

Facial expressions are an important communication channel and are widely used by humans [15]. As a way to express them non-verbally, they are used for both, pain and emotions [6,8]. In the former, it may signal a plea for help and for the latter, it can be used to reveal the current emotional state of a person.

A systematic way of describing a facial expression is the *Facial Action Coding System (FACS)* developed by Ekman et al. [7]. It defines so-called *Action Units (AUs)* which correspond to an elementary movement of the face, i.e. a distinct visual display. Each AU has an associated code, name an is noted with an intensity value. Complex facial expressions are composed of multiple AUs.

Here, we are using OpenFace 2.0 [2], a freely available toolkit for research purposes, to automatically extract intensity values (normalized to the range $[0; 1]$) for 16 different AUs from the videos.

OpenFace uses a *Multi-task Convolutional Neural Network* [32] to find the face in the image, detects facial landmarks by incorporating a mixture of experts model [13] in a neural network hierarchy and tracks them over the video sequence. Based on these landmarks, geometric (modelled via Point Distribution Models [3]) and appearance features (*Histogram of Oriented Gradients* from image patches) are calculated to train a *Support Vector Regression* model which results in different intensity values.

As features, we compute the AU intensities for all subject videos. In order to reduce the noise in the data, we smooth the intensities with a Butterworth filter (first order, 1Hz cutoff frequency). We also observed different baseline levels for AUs and subjects (the intensities start at different levels). As a countermeasure, we normalize the features by subtracting the median intensity of the first k frames (with e.g. $k = 5$) and clip the result

$$\tilde{a}_i = \max\left(a_i - \mathrm{median}\left(a_{i,1}, a_{i,2}, \ldots, a_{i,k}\right), 0\right). \tag{1}$$

The vector $a_i = (a_{i,1}, a_{i,2}, \ldots, a_{i,n})$ contains the intensities for the i-th AU and all n frames of the video. The underlying assumption is that it is likely that the first few frames of a video contain a neutral expression and any noticeable intensities are hence due to baseline variations. As a result, the intensity values start closer at zero. The median is used because it is less sensitive against outliers and the clipping prevents negative intensity values.

The emotion videos are downsampled to 138 frames to match with the length of the videos of part A and the responses of all neutral and pain videos are averaged together so that the number of videos is the same across classes. In total, this results in a $7 \times 16 \times 64 \times 138$ tensor (classes, AUs, subjects and time dimensions). In the following, we operate on this tensor and create different visualizations.

4 Feature Visualizations

4.1 Total Action Unit Intensities per Class

We combine the subject and time dimensions and show the intensities for each AU and class in a matrix (Fig. 1). In the first row, the responses of the neutral class are depicted which are relatively low in general, although, not zero. This is probably due to some noise in the data (e.g. because of detection errors). However, the responses are still different from the other classes.

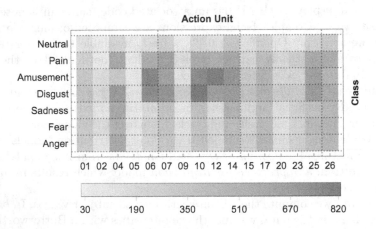

Fig. 1. Total AU intensity for each of the seven classes and 16 AUs (denoted with the code). Responses over time and subjects are combined. Mappings from the AU code to the respective name can e.g. be found in Fig. 3.

The pain, amusement and disgust classes show clear responses for some AUs. However, the overlap is high which means that, at least to some degree, the same AUs were displayed by the subjects. A noticeable exception is the *Brow Lowerer (AU04)* which mainly occurs in the pain and disgust classes but less in the amusement class. Overall, the responses for the pain class are a bit lower than for the amusement and disgust classes. This may be explained by Fig. 6, i.e. some subjects showed only little reactions to the heat stimulus.

Sadness, fear and anger are the remaining three emotion classes and they do not show a clear AU pattern. What is more, there are only a few differences between the classes. The *Brow Lowerer (AU04)* is, again, an exception. It has relatively high responses for all three classes. This AU alone is not necessarily an indication for an emotion [6] and may be explained otherwise. For example, when the subjects were watching the film clips, they were perhaps irritated about something which had happened in the clip and hence showed a small sign of confusion or lack of understanding. In total, it seems as if these emotions could not be induced to the subjects successfully.

4.2 Dependency Graphs

In this section, we visualize not only the intensities of AUs but also their dependencies, i.e. the joint usage of each pair of AUs. This is done by constructing a weighted graph $G = (N, E)$ where each node in N denotes an AU and each edge in E denotes the co-occurrence of two AUs. The crucial part is the calculation of the edge weights. A weight should be high when two AUs are used often and intensely together over time. To model this, we propose to use a correlation measure based on the point-wise matrix multiplication

$$e_{ij} = \sum_{n=1}^{64} \sum_{m=1}^{138} (T_t(A_i) \odot T_t(A_j))_{n,m} \tag{2}$$

$$T_t(A) = \left(\begin{cases} 0, & a_{ij} \leq t \\ a_{ij}, & a_{ij} > t \end{cases} \right)_{\substack{1 \leq i \leq 64 \\ 1 \leq j \leq 138}} \tag{3}$$

with e_{ij} denoting the weight between the i-th and j-th AUs, A_i the 64×138 matrix containing the intensities of the i-th AU for all subjects over time and $\odot$ denotes the point-wise matrix multiplication. $T_t(A)$ applies a threshold to the matrix A which sets all matrix elements a_{ij} with an intensity lower than or equal to t to zero. $(A)_{n,m}$ selects the component in the n-th row and m-th column of the matrix A.

Equation 2 basically compares the AU responses over time and then aggregates the result. This concept is also visualized in Fig. 2. The idea of the multiplication is that an AU pair contributes only to an edge weight when the responses for both AUs are high.

In the following, we show the graph for the pain, amusement and disgust classes. The other three emotion classes are not shown since they have no clear AU pattern (cf. Fig. 1).

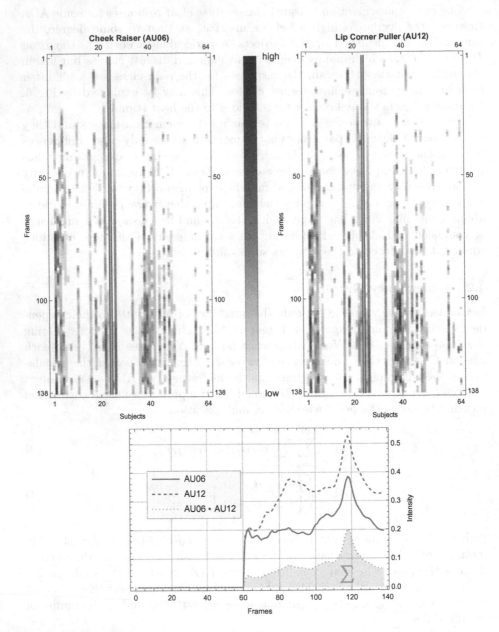

Fig. 2. Example of the edge weight calculation. The two matrix plots show the (thresholded) AU responses for all subjects over time for two AUs. In both plots, the responses of two subjects are highlighted and shown enlarged in the bottom plot which visualizes the multiplication of the AU responses over time. This result is then added up to arrive at a scalar edge weight for each AU pair. The threshold is set to $t = 0.15$.

General. Before discussing the individual graphs, some general remarks first. It is expected that two AUs share a strong connection when both have overall high intensities in general. This is because when a node has a high average intensity, it is likely that it occurred frequently and two such nodes are predestined to also co-occur together.

Figure 3, 4 and 5 show the graphs for the three emotion classes in question. When comparing all graphs, it is noticeable that there is some overlap between the classes. This is true for the nodes (like it also was the case in Fig. 1) but also for some edges. For example, all three graphs have a relatively strong[1] edge between the *Cheek Raiser (AU06)* and the *Lip Corner Puller (AU12)*. However, the absolute scaling is still different and each graph has its own edge pattern (the set of dominant edges).

Pain Graph. The dependency graph for the pain class is visualized in Fig. 3. The most dominant node is the *Lid Tightener (AU07)* and it has strong connections to the *Cheek Raiser (AU06)* and the *Upper Lip Raiser (AU10)* which also share a strong connection. Further, the *Lip Corner Puller (AU12)* and the *Lips Part (AU25)* are also strongly connected to the nodes. These five nodes seem to be important for the typical pain face and this is also in consistency with the AUs typically associated with a painful expression [17].

A node with a relatively high intensity but only weak connections is the *Brow Lowerer (AU04)*. It is sometimes used together with the *Lid Tightener (AU07)* but otherwise has only a few joint usages. It was maybe only shown by subjects which reacted mildly to the heat stimulus resulting in little to no change of the visual display except for a small notice that something had happened.

The *Jaw Drop (AU26)* node has a medium intensity with the strongest connection to the *Lips Part (AU25)* even though the *Lid Tightener (AU07)* occurs with the highest intensity in general. This may be explained by the physical proximity of AU25 and AU26 in the face. That is, opening up the lips leads almost inevitably to a drop of the jaw (visually speaking).

Amusement Graph. Figure 4 visualizes the graph for the videos of the amusement class. The two strongest nodes are the *Cheek Raiser (AU06)* as well as the *Lip Corner Puller (AU12)* and they share a strong connection. These are also the AUs commonly associated with an amusement expression [9]. At least for some subjects, this emotion was successfully induced.

The *Upper Lip Raiser (AU10)* and the *Lips Part (AU25)* occur also sometimes with the two AUs mentioned. They may be part of extreme expressions (laughter) where the mouth of the subject is also open.

Disgust Graph. In Fig. 5, the dependency graph of the disgust class is shown. Now, the node with the highest intensity is the *Upper Lip Raiser (AU10)* with a strong connection to the *Cheek Raiser (AU06)*. Both AUs are, strictly speaking,

---

[1] Relative to the edge weights in each graph. Cf. the different edge scaling.

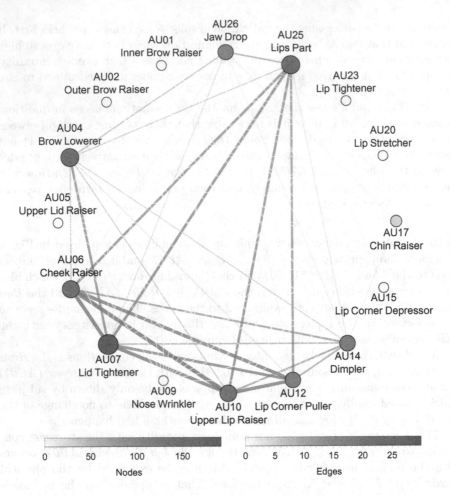

Fig. 3. Dependency graph of the pain class. Each node represents an AU and the edges between the AUs the join usage. The edge weight is calculated via Eq. 2 (see also Fig. 2) and depicted by the thickness and colour of the edges. The nodes are styled according to the overall intensity of the AUs (via the colour and the circle size) similar to Fig. 1.

not part of the set of AUs commonly associated with a disgust expression [9]. However, the *Nose Wrinkler (AU09)* is on the list and since it is visually related to the *Upper Lip Raiser (AU10)*[2], it is likely that they got confused in the detection process.

There are also AUs present in the disgust graph which are more related to an amusement expression. For example, the *Lip Corner Puller (AU12)* and the *Dimpler (AU14)*, both with connections to the *Cheek Raiser (AU06)*. This may indicate that subjects actually showed amusement expressions while they were

---

[2] Wrinkling of the nose tends to also raise the upper lip at least to some degree.

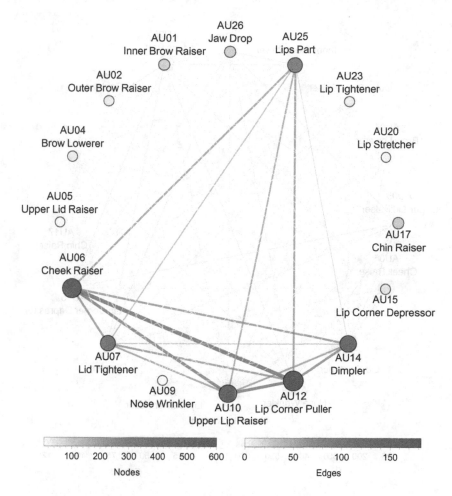

Fig. 4. Dependency graph of the amusement class (similar to Fig. 3).

watching the film clips either because they glossed over their disgust feelings with an amusement expression or they were actually amused by the clip (some subjects did rate the disgust clips as (slightly) amusing [33]).

4.3 Differences Across Subjects

We also want to show how the subjects in the database differ in their reactions to the stimuli (pain or emotion). For this, Fig. 6 shows the individual subject responses over time for three classes arranged in a grid.

For the neutral class, the responses are generally low and this is also expected. However, there are still some subjects with noticeable intensities (e.g. fourth row, fourth column) for this class. This can be seen by the slightly increased mean line and the relatively high standard deviation. This may be due to subjects

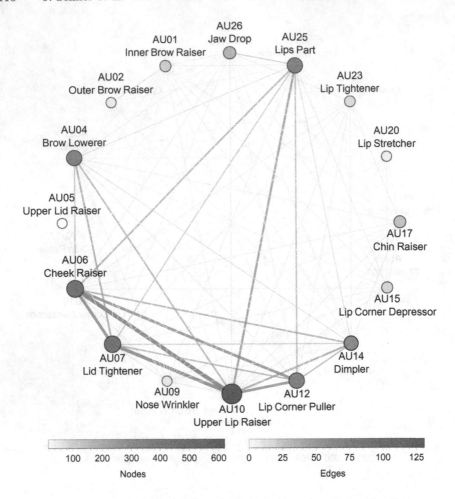

Fig. 5. Dependency graph of the disgust class (similar to Fig. 3).

which were showing (arbitrary) expressions in the pause phases. For example, it is possible that they were still recovering from the previous heat phase as also reported by Werner et al. [30].

The responses for the pain class varies heavily across subjects. While there are subjects with very high intensities (e.g. first row, second column), there are others who reacted only mildly to the heat stimulus (e.g. ninth row, fourth column). It is not to be expected that any classifier can discriminate between the classes when the responses are not sufficiently different.

If the AU intensities of a subject are high, the general pattern of the AU curves is that they first increase and then decrease again. This is because the heat stimulus is only active during the first $\approx$ 80 frames of the videos and it requires some time until the heat induction has an effect [30].

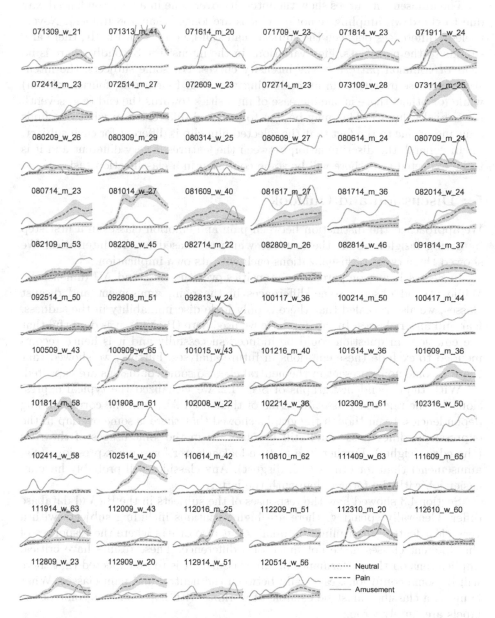

Fig. 6. Intensity values for each subject over time for three classes (neutral, pain and amusement). Only one emotion class is shown to avoid too much clutter. The mean over all AUs is depicted as lines and the shaded area denotes 0.25 standard deviation from the corresponding mean (reduced for better distinguishability). The information about the standard deviation is only depicted for the neutral and pain classes since here 20 videos are available.

The amusement curves show the intensity over time in a very condensed way due to the downsampling (emotion videos are longer than 138 frames). Nevertheless, differences between the subjects can still be observed. Firstly, there are, similar to the pain class, high variations in the intensities. Secondly, there is no clear or common pattern of the intensity curves. For some subjects, the intensities increase over time in an oscillating way (e.g. fourth row, fourth column) while for others there is one increase of intensities towards the end (e.g. seventh row, third column). This may be due to personal differences in what one finds amusing or due to the fact that the selected film clip is different for each subject.

In general, the discrimination between the features is very different and it is to be expected that there will be some confusion in a classification task.

5   Discussion and Outlook

We approached the distinction between pain and emotion classes in a first step by giving insights about the features which are based on AU intensities. We showed three types of visualizations each with its own implication.

In Sect. 4.1, we compared the intensities over the class and AU dimensions. While we did observe some differences in the pain, amusement and disgust classes, we also revealed that there is only little discriminability in the sadness, fear and anger classes. In the database we used here (BioVid), it is doubtful that the emotions in question could be induced successfully and it is hence recommended to exclude these emotions in future analyses. Further, we showed that there is some noise present in the neutral class so some confusions are expected.

With the dependency graphs of Sect. 4.2, we visualized the typical expressions for the relevant classes in terms of their used AUs and the corresponding dependencies. Even though the graphs showed that there is some overlap in the expressions, differences could still be observed in the joint usages of the AUs (the edge weights). Further, the picture looks clearer for some expressions (e.g. amusement) than for others (e.g. disgust). Any classifier will probably have an easier job with the former than with the latter.

Section 4.3 showed how the responses of the subjects in the BioVid database differ. Generally speaking, there are high variations including subjects with a very clear feature discrimination quality but also others where the responses of the different classes make not much of a difference. These results have critical implications on the performance of any classifier. It is to be expected that there will be some confusions, especially between the neutral and pain classes. What is more, a classifier must be capable of working with noisy data as some of the labels are simply wrong.

As next steps, we plan to use the data of the relevant classes (neutral, pain, amusement and disgust) and asses them in a classification task. For this, special attention to the emotion classes is required as there is only one video per emotion available (compared to the 20 videos in the neutral and pain classes), i.e. a high class imbalance. Further, the emotion videos are of different length and an approach needs to be developed to compare them with the neutral and pain videos (which have always the same length).

Regarding the general question whether it is (easily) possible to distinguish between pain and emotions, further data must be collected. This is especially true for the sadness, fear and anger classes as the BioVid database does not allow to make clear statements. Ideally, the data is collected in real-world scenarios enriched with fine-grained labels.

References

1. The biovid heat pain database. http://www.iikt.ovgu.de/BioVid.html
2. Baltrušaitis, T., Zadeh, A., Lim, Y.C., Morency, L.P.: Openface 2.0: facial behavior analysis toolkit. In: 2018 13th IEEE International Conference on Automatic Face Gesture Recognition (FG 2018), pp. 59–66 (2018). https://doi.org/10.1109/FG. 2018.00019
3. Cootes, T.F., Taylor, C.J., Cooper, D.H., Graham, J.R.: Active shape models-their training and application. Comput. Vis. Image Underst. **61**(1), 38–59. https://doi. org/10.1006/cviu.1995.1004
4. Craig, K.D., Prkachin, K.M., Grunau, R.E.: The facial expression of pain. In: Turk, D.C., Melzack, R. (eds.) Handbook of Pain Assessment, pp. 153–169. Guilford Press, New York (2001)
5. De la Torre, F., Cohn, J.F.: Facial expression analysis. In: Moeslund, T.B., Hilton, A., Krüger, V., Sigal, L. (eds.) Visual Analysis of Humans: Looking at People, pp. 377–409. Springer, London (2001). https://doi.org/10.1007/978-0-85729-997-0_19
6. Ekman, P.: Emotions revealed. 2nd owl books edn. Owl Books, New York. http:// www.loc.gov/catdir/enhancements/fy0733/2007277266-b.html
7. Ekman, P., Friesen, W.V., Hager, J.C.: Facial Action Coding System. Research Nexus, Salt Lake City (2002)
8. Ekman, P., Friesen, W.V., O'Sullivan, M., Scherer, K.: Relative importance of face, body, and speech in judgments of personality and affect. J. Pers. Soc. Psychol. **38**(2). https://doi.org/10.1037/0022-3514.38.2.270.
9. Friesen, W.V., Ekman, P.: EMFACS-7, California
10. Hadjistavropoulos, T., Craig, K.D.: Pain: Psychological Perspectives. 1st edn. Lawrence Erlbaum Associates, Publishers (2004)
11. Hale, C.J., Hadjistavropoulos, T.: Emotional components of pain. Pain Res. Manag. **2**(4). https://doi.org/10.1155/1997/283582
12. Hammal, Z., Kunz, M.: Pain monitoring: a dynamic and context-sensitive system. Pattern Recognit. **45**(4), 1265–1280 (2012). https://doi.org/10.1016/j.patcog.2011. 09.014, http://www.sciencedirect.com/science/article/pii/S0031320311003931
13. Hauskrecht, M.: Ensamble methods mixtures of experts. https://people.cs.pitt. edu/~milos/courses/cs2750-Spring04/lectures/class22.pdf
14. LeResche, L., Dworkin, S.F.: Facial expressions of pain and emotions in chronic TMD patients. Pain **35**(1), 71–78. https://doi.org/10.1016/0304-3959(88)90278-3, http://www.sciencedirect.com/science/article/pii/0304395988902783
15. Mehrabian, A.: Communication without words. Psychol. Today **2**(4), 53–56 (1968)
16. Niese, R., Al-Hamadi, A., Panning, A., Brammen, D.G., Ebmeyer, U., Michaelis, B.: Towards pain recognition in post-operative phases using 3D-based features from video and support vector machines. JDCTA **3**, 21–33 (2009)
17. Prkachin, K.M.: The consistency of facial expressions of pain: a comparison across modalities. In: Ekman, P., Rosenberg, E.L. (eds.) What the Face Reveals, pp. 181–198. Oxford University Press. https://doi.org/10.1093/acprof:oso/9780195179644. 003.0009

18. Sariyanidi, E., Gunes, H., Cavallaro, A.: Automatic analysis of facial affect. IEEE Trans. Pattern Anal. Mach. Intell. **37**(6), 1113–1133. https://doi.org/10.1109/TPAMI.2014.2366127

19. Simon, D., Craig, K.D., Gosselin, F., Belin, P., Rainville, P.: Recognition and discrimination of prototypical dynamic expressions of pain and emotions. PAIN® **135**(1), 55–64 (2008). https://doi.org/10.1016/j.pain.2007.05.008, http://www.sciencedirect.com/science/article/pii/S0304395907002485

20. Sumathi, C.: Automatic facial expression analysis a survey. Int. J. Comput. Sci. Eng. Surv. **3**(6), 47–59. https://doi.org/10.5121/ijcses.2012.3604

21. Thiam, P., Kächele, M., Schwenker, F., Palm, G.: Ensembles of support vector data description for active learning based annotation of affective corpora. In: 2015 IEEE Symposium Series on Computational Intelligence, pp. 1801–1807, December 2015

22. Thiam, P., et al.: Multi-modal pain intensity recognition based on the senseemotion database. IEEE Trans. Affect. Comput. (2019). https://doi.org/10.1109/TAFFC.2019.2892090

23. Thiam, P., Kessler, V., Schwenker, F.: Hierarchical combination of video features for personalised pain level recognition. In: Proceedings of the 25th European Symposium of Artificial Neural Networks, Computational Intelligence and Machine Learning, pp. 465–470 (2017)

24. Thiam, P., Kessler, V., Walter, S., Palm, G., Schwenker, F.: Audio-visual recognition of pain intensity. In: Schwenker, F., Scherer, S. (eds.) MPRSS 2016. LNCS (LNAI), vol. 10183, pp. 110–126. Springer, Cham (2017). https://doi.org/10.1007/978-3-319-59259-6_10

25. Thiam, P., Meudt, S., Kächele, M., Palm, G., Schwenker, F.: Detection of emotional events utilizing support vector methods in an active learning HCI scenario. In: Proceedings of the 2014 Workshop on Emotion Representation and Modelling in Human-Computer-Interaction-Systems, ERM4HCI 2014, pp. 31–36. ACM, New York (2014)

26. Thiam, P., Meudt, S., Palm, G., Schwenker, F.: A temporal dependency based multi-modal active learning approach for audiovaudio event detection. Neural Process. Lett. **48**(2), 709–732 (2018)

27. Walter, S., et al.: The biovid heat pain database data for the advancement and systematic validation of an automated pain recognition system. In: 2013 IEEE International Conference on Cybernetics (CYBCO), pp. 128–131. IEEE. https://doi.org/10.1109/CYBConf.2013.6617456

28. Werner, P., Al-Hamadi, A., Limbrecht-Ecklundt, K., Walter, S., Gruss, S., Traue, H.C.: Automatic pain assessment with facial activity descriptors. IEEE Trans. Affect. Comput. **8**(3), 286–299. https://doi.org/10.1109/TAFFC.2016.2537327

29. Werner, P., Al-Hamadi, A., Niese, R., Walter, S., Gruss, S., Traue, H.: Towards pain monitoring: Facial expression, head pose, a new database, an automatic system and remaining challenges. In: Burghardt, T., Damen, D., Mayol-Cuevas, W., Mirmehdi, M. (eds.) Proceedings of the British Machine Vision Conference 2013, pp. 119.1–119.13. British Machine Vision Association. https://doi.org/10.5244/C.27.119

30. Werner, P., Al-Hamadi, A., Walter, S.: Analysis of facial expressiveness during experimentally induced heat pain. In: 2017 Seventh International Conference on Affective Computing and Intelligent Interaction Workshops and Demos (ACIIW), pp. 176–180. IEEE. https://doi.org/10.1109/ACIIW.2017.8272610

31. Zeng, Z., Pantic, M., Roisman, G.I., Huang, T.S.: A survey of affect recognition methods: audio, visual, and spontaneous expressions. IEEE Trans. Pattern Anal. Mach. Intell. **31**(1), 39–58. https://doi.org/10.1109/TPAMI.2008.52

32. Zhang, K., Zhang, Z., Li, Z., Qiao, Y.: Joint face detection and alignment using multi-task cascaded convolutional networks. IEEE Signal Process. Lett. **23**(10), 1499–1503. https://doi.org/10.1109/LSP.2016.2603342
33. Zhang, L., et al.: "BioVid Emo DB": A multimodal database for emotion analyses validated by subjective ratings. In: 2016 IEEE Symposium Series on Computational Intelligence (SSCI), pp. 1–6. IEEE. https://doi.org/10.1109/SSCI.2016.7849931

Author Index

Printed in the United States
By Bookmasters